Julia's Cats

Julia's Cats

JULIA CHILD'S LIFE
in THE COMPANY *of* CATS

PATRICIA BAREY *and* THERESE BURSON

ABRAMS IMAGE, NEW YORK

Editor: David Cashion
Designer: Darilyn Lowe Carnes
Production Manager: Ankur Ghosh

Library of Congress Cataloging-in-Publication Data

Barey, Patricia.
 Julia's cats : Julia Child's life in the company of cats / Patricia Barey, Therese Burson.
   p. cm.
 ISBN 978-1-4197-0275-4 (hardback)
 1. Child, Julia. 2. Women cat owners—United States—Biography. 3. Cats—Anecdotes.
 4. Cooks—United States—Biography. I. Burson, Therese. II. Title.
 SF442.82.C55B37 2013
 636.80092'2—dc23
                          2012004512

Text copyright © 2012 Patricia Barey and Therese Burson

Recipe on page 144 from FROM JULIA CHILD'S KITCHEN by Julia Child, copyright
© 1975 by Julia Child. Used by permission of Alfred A. Knopf, a division of Random
House, Inc.

All the photos reproduced in this book, with the exception of those listed below,
are by Paul Child and published with permission from the Schlesinger Library, Radcliffe
Institute, Harvard University. Paul Child photos and images on pages 21, 31, 37, 53,
and 112 © The Julia Child Foundation for Gastronomy and the Culinary Arts.

Additional photos provided with permission and courtesy of the following:
Sandy Shepard/collection of Rosemary Manell (page 10), Zoom-zoom/Dreamstime.com
(page 12), Manuel Freres/Hulton Archive/Getty Images (page 22), private collection
(page 28), Maggie Mah Johnson (page 32), the family of Julia Child (page 85), Brian
Leatart (page 103), Jim Scherer (page 116), David Nussbaum (page 132).

Printed and bound in the U.S.A.
10 9 8 7 6 5 4 3 2 1

Abrams Image books are available at special discounts when purchased in quantity for
premiums and promotions as well as fundraising or educational use. Special editions can
also be created to specification. For details, contact specialsales@abramsbooks.com or
the address below.

THE ART OF BOOKS SINCE 1949
115 West 18th Street
New York, NY 10011
www.abramsbooks.com

Frontispiece:
Julia Child with copper cat. Photo by Paul Child, 1964

CONTENTS

A REPORTER ONCE ASKED Julia Child what she might whip up for her creator when she got to heaven. Julia wasn't a religious person—she believed heaven was right here on earth, in her own cozy kitchen, hovering over a skillet sizzling with shallots and butter, then sitting down to share a meal with people she loved, a cat wrapped around her ankles, meowing for treats.

She lost count of how often she'd been quizzed about what she wanted for her own last meal. She once composed a detailed menu that left nothing to chance: Begin with Cotuit oysters on thinly sliced and buttered homemade rye bread. Caviar and vodka, then fresh green California asparagus. For the main course, her favorite duck recipe, "the one in which you roast the duck until the breast is rare and then cook the legs and wings separately *en confit*, with a very nice light port wine sauce." Serve it with peas and *pommes Anna* and a big Burgundy or Saint-Émilion from a very good year. Crusty French bread, of course. Follow the entrée with lettuce and endive dressed with lemon and French olive oil. A classic creamy dessert, Charlotte Malakoff, paired with an ambrosial Château d'Yquem. Top off the meal with some ripe grapes, a Comice pear, perhaps chocolate truffles with the coffee and liqueurs.

As time went on, she came to see the question about her final meal as beside the point. The menu she would choose didn't really matter as long as it was *soigné*—prepared with respect for the ingredients and the process, cooked with care and presented with love.

In the summer of 2004, Julia had been in failing health following complications from knee surgery, and after a brief hospitalization, she refused further treatment for a massive infection. She wanted to be at home, having decided her time had come to "slip off the raft." One August night, just four days before her ninety-second birthday, she asked her longtime assistant to make a batch of soup. Stephanie took down Julia's own copy of *Mastering the Art of French Cooking* and opened it to page forty-three. She knew the recipe by heart but wanted "The Book" nearby. Soon a cloud of rich scents rising from the bubbling beef stock and onions sautéing in butter—lots of butter—filled the apartment.

The fragrant aroma worked its magic. Julia savored the bowl of her own French onion soup. A beloved dinner companion that night was a wild little black-and-white kitten named Minou, who shared Julia's home in a retirement community near Santa Barbara. Full of feline joie de vivre, Minou was the soul mate who brightened Julia's days. When she was ready for bed, the kitten curled up in his customary spot on the right side of the pillow. Minou kept watch through the night as Julia's charmed life ebbed away, where she said it all truly began, in the company of cats.

I.

LA BELLE FRANCE:
A NEW LIFE BEGINS

THIRTY-SIX-YEAR-OLD newlywed Julia Child was feeling queasy as she peered out the porthole of a heaving SS *America*. There were no stars in the November sky, but she could make out dim lights winking through the grimy fog. Julia's first glimpse of France made sleep impossible, so she bent over her tiny writing table and added a note to the letter her husband, Paul, was writing to his twin brother, Charlie, back in Pennsylvania.

She tells everyone that she misses them terribly but can't wait to finally see Paris. She sends her love especially to the family dog and Mimi, her favorite cat-in-law. She pleads for news of their latest mischief.

Julia had married into a letter-writing, animal-loving family that warmly embraced its dogs and cats, and the tall, two-legged newcomer with the warbly voice. Cold noses, sloppy dog kisses, and purring balls of fur were highlights of every family reunion. They reminded her of growing up in a rambunctious Pasadena household where frisky Airedales were the favorite playmates of Julia and her two siblings.

A passion for animals was one more sign—if she needed any more—that her marriage to Paul would be a good match. They also shared an appetite for fine food and adventure. They fell in love over steaming bowls of potted chicken in Kunming, China, where they were both stationed during the war while working for the Office of Strategic Services, America's first spy agency.

Paul Child was ten years older—and ten inches shorter—than Julia. He worked for the Foreign Service and in the fall of 1948 was heading for his new job designing cultural exhibits at the American embassy in Paris. A talented photographer, painter, and poet, Paul had lived in a very different Paris twenty

A love match: Julia and Paul

years earlier, when Americans came by the boatload to pen great thoughts in cafés and party the nights away in jazz clubs. Now he was eager to show his wide-eyed California bride, Julia McWilliams, the Paris he so loved. She jumped at the chance to live in the most beautiful city in the world.

Dawn was just breaking as burly stevedores wrestled with six trunks and fourteen suitcases, jammed with almost everything the couple owned, and lowered their massive Buick to the dock. The "Blue Flash" guzzled petrol at a breathtaking rate and would be a tight fit in the narrow streets of the Left Bank where they planned to settle, but it was a gift from Julia's father they couldn't afford to leave behind.

They squeezed into the front seat, giddy with fatigue and anticipation. Paul revved the engine and aimed for Paris. On the French country roads, tiny Citroëns and Renaults were dwarfed by the Flash, like pilot fish around a huge blue shark. Julia's head swiveled from the map to the window as she breathlessly pointed out every gabled farmhouse and church spire. Paul figured they'd see the City of Light by nightfall, even with a stop in Rouen for lunch.

THEY RUMBLED INTO the medieval town hungry, looking for la Couronne, a restaurant Paul picked out of his dog-eared *Guide Michelin*. The wood-beamed room was cozy and warm, and a low fire licked at three fat ducks slowly rotating on a spit. The air was dense with the scent of bubbling butter as they followed a waiter to their table and pored over the menu. Julia deferred to Paul, who seemed to know it by heart. Start with oysters *portugaises* on buttered rounds of rye. Then a whole Dover sole, faintly briny, from that morning's catch, still sizzling on the plate, followed by a crisp green salad, *fromage blanc*, and strong filtered coffee. They shared a bottle of chilled Pouilly-Fuissé— in the middle of the day! Julia felt tipsily French already.

Her first bite of French food was a revelation—she remembered it for the rest of her life, and the memory grew more delicious every time she told the story.

They arrived in Paris as the sun was setting. Through the windshield lay a city Paul scarcely recognized. Piles of rubble clogged some streets and few cars snaked through the normally teeming traffic circles. Whole blocks of apartment buildings were dark, boulevards all but deserted. Gas was still scarce and electricity unreliable. Unable to get butter and cream, chefs at some of the fancier restaurants closed their doors rather than compromise their haute-cuisine standards. Cuisine of any kind was hard to come by for many Parisians, let alone the abandoned cats and dogs who roamed the city scrounging for food and warmth. When there were no table scraps, the ranks of gutter cats, the city's renowned *chats de gouttières*, skittered along slate rooftops, hoping to snare dozing pigeons.

Paul gripped the wheel tightly, cranked down the window,

and leaned out to get a better view. Like other drivers he turned off his headlights, a cautionary habit left over from the war years, and slowly maneuvered the Flash through cramped streets in the murky dusk. Occasionally, shadowy figures emerged from the gloom, making driving even more unnerving.

As they peered through the windshield, suddenly there it was—*la tour Eiffel*, outlined in red blinking lights, another reminder of the city's vulnerability during the war. Julia's heart exploded at the sight.

THE FIRST MONTH, they stayed at the Hôtel Pont Royal, a snazzy address in the Latin Quarter, while Paul settled into his job at the embassy and Julia searched for an apartment. She finally found one at 81 rue de l'Université, in the most elegant quarter of Paris. Although the old *hôtel particulier* oozed Gallic charm, it had seen better days and definitely lacked American amenities, like dependable heat and electricity. Some nights as they sat reading in the dim salon, they could see their breath. The formal but shabby Louis XVI decor made them feel as though they should be wearing powdered wigs.

The apartment was stuffed with bric-a-brac, faded draperies, and too many rickety tables and chairs, so they moved the most unsightly pieces to a storage room they called the *oubliette*, the "forgettery." The drafty, high-ceilinged rooms quickly swallowed the contents of their many trunks and suitcases. They were glad they'd brought all those extra blankets, sheets, and warm clothing, since scarcity was still a painful fact of French life.

As they settled in, Julia and Paul found that the warmest spot was the top-floor kitchen, up a narrow back staircase from the living rooms. Originally servants' quarters, the kitchen had large windows facing the courtyard, so it was bright even on dreary mornings. And fairly spacious, though Julia towered over everything in it except for an ancient stove, a coal-burning "monster" that made her long for the modern kitchen she had left behind in their house on Olive Street in Washington, D.C. On one of her first shopping forays, she bought a compact gas stove with two small ovens on spindly legs, which they wedged next to the behemoth. The shallow soapstone sink

Roo de Loo view: Paris in winter

that supplied cold running water, when the pipes didn't freeze, just wouldn't do. So she devised a makeshift hot-water system for dishwashing and warm baths, and insisted on covered containers for garbage. Roughing it at the family cabin in Maine was one thing, but she refused to put up with primitive conditions in the cultural capital of the world.

It took some getting used to, but "Roo de Loo," as Julia named it, gradually became home.

The view was dazzling—the Paris of her dreams. The windows overlooked the courtyard of the Ministry of Defense, and the graceful spires of the Church of Saint Clotilde floated above the rooftops, its bell softly singing the hours. It was all very picturesque, except that winter, foggy and damp, was settling in around the gray stone buildings. Everyone in Paris was looking for warmth, especially the mice.

TO JULIA'S SURPRISE, Roo de Loo came with a maid—
and mice in the kitchen. Neither woman could tolerate *souris*
scampering among the pots and pans, so one rainy day the
frizzy-haired *femme de ménage* bumped up the kitchen stairs
with a large market basket on her arm. Could a warm brioche,
a spicy country pâté, *pain au chocolat,* or some other delectable
edible be inside? No, this basket held something more
delicious. Jeanne lifted the lid, and a black-and-mud-colored
ball of fur emerged. Two glittering green eyes traveled up
and up and up until they met Julia's. A pussycat! It was love at
first sight.

Jeanne patiently explained that French housewives
relied on cats to control the mice, and they usually just called
them Minou (Pussy). She shrugged and left Julia gazing at her
adorable new mousetrap. The cat stared back but couldn't be
coaxed from the basket. When Julia finally gave up and went
to stir her simmering stockpot, the kitty's curiosity took over,
and it leaped to a shelf above the stove and crouched next to
a mixing bowl.

When Paul returned from the embassy for lunch, as
he did most days, they embraced as if they'd been apart for
months, not a few hours. Julia gleefully introduced him to
Minou, the *purrrrfect* answer to their mouse-control problem.
Paul studied the newcomer carefully and delivered some
interesting news—Monsieur Pussycat was a mademoiselle.
Without missing a beat, Julia rechristened her "Minette" and
set two steaming bowls of soup on the table.

She had been bending over her stove all morning trying
to duplicate the velvety mushroom soup they had devoured at

New arrival

their favorite restaurant the night before. She pulled a baguette from Paul's raincoat pocket, tore the crusty loaf into chunks, and sliced big wedges of strong-smelling Roquefort. She filled two tumblers from an open bottle of red wine and joined Paul at the table, fretting about the potage. It smelled scrumptious, but was full of lumps. Maybe it was the roux—was it hot broth added to flour paste, or the other way around? Paul took a spoonful, paused, then let his diplomatic training kick into gear. Lumpy, but still very tasty. He kissed her hand and told her not to worry so much. Julia vowed to try again even if it took all afternoon. Paul, sensing another chance to show husbandly support, volunteered to be her guinea pig and taste every batch.

From her safe perch, the hungry cat watched and waited. Finally, she bounded to the floor and onto Paul's lap. From under the table's edge, her nose rested just inches from his bowl and the crumbled cheese on the plate. With one flick of her paw, she scooped a chunk into her mouth, then eyed the bowl of soup.

Julia took the hint, spooned some soup into a saucer, and set it on the floor. She watched anxiously, worried that even a starving cat might find her soup wanting. At first Minette ignored the soup, seeming content on Paul's lap. Suddenly she slid to the floor, dipped a delicate paw into the soup, and raised a lump to her mouth, chewed deliberately, then lapped the saucer until it gleamed. Paul marveled at Minette's elegant French airs while Julia refilled the saucer—and their bowls. A drowsy pussycat studied her reflection in the empty dish, then rested her head on Julia's large red leather shoe as the murmuring voices lulled her to sleep.

The mice scurrying under the sink had little to fear— Minette had other menu options.

MÉNAGE À TROIS

WITH THE MOUSE patrol more or less in place, Minette quickly became an indispensable member of the Child household during the chilly winter of 1949. The furry newbie was loaded with personality. Sly. Curious. Tireless, unless suddenly overcome with the urge to nap. Clever and resourceful, she was an endless source of amusement. Paul and Julia had always loved animals but never thought of themselves as "cat people," so falling head over heels for Minette took them both quite by surprise.

The snug kitchen was the trio's favorite hub. To make it her own, Julia hung some favorite cooking tools—a Magnagrip knife holder and a Dazey can opener. Back home, her beginner's *batterie de cuisine* seemed adequate, but here she began to covet the balloon whisks, wooden paddles, and tortoiseshell scrapers she saw in the shops. Were these the magic wands that transformed ordinary ingredients into sublime dishes? She was determined to find out.

Breakfast was still very American: eggs and toast, and coffee brewed in the battered tin percolator. Coffee remained a hot item on the black market, but Julia could get hers from the American commissary. Like most old Parisian apartments, theirs had no refrigerator, and on winter mornings when the air was colder outside, they kept a bottle of milk on the window ledge. The cream rose to the top overnight, a special treat Paul and Julia indulgently scooped into Minette's dish, until they discovered it gave her *crise de foie* (digestive troubles).

Julia went off to Berlitz classes three mornings a week, then rushed home to make lunch for Paul and maybe steal a little snuggling time. Afternoons she wandered the streets of the *quartier*, map and French phrase book in hand. Minette was content to sit by the large windows in the curved hallway that joined the wings of the L-shaped apartment. There she stared out over the green slate rooftops of Paris shrouded in fog. On damp winter days, pigeons cooing under the dripping eaves set her teeth to chattering.

When Julia returned from her afternoon jaunts, she often found Minette in the kitchen sitting next to her preferred toy, a long piece of string with a gnawed brussels sprout tied to its end, patiently waiting for a playmate. Sometimes she seemed spellbound by something, anything, even dust bunnies beneath the cold stove. Nothing could break her Zen-like concentration—unless Julia dangled a fat sausage from her market basket and was willing to share. On rare occasions Minette pranced into the kitchen, head high in the air, to deposit a hapless and no doubt very slow mouse. Paul figured this display of hunting prowess was an attempt to prove she was earning her keep. But all three of them knew Minette's place was secure—she had them at "Meow."

Ready to play

EVENINGS, JULIA, PAUL, and Minette huddled around a
potbellied stove in the drafty salon. Julia, swaddled in a long
woolen scarf and tweed coat buttoned to the collar, fumbled
the pages of her Berlitz with gloved hands. A shivering
Paul leafed through stacks of photographs and maps for an
exhibition on the Berlin airlift, his first major project for the
US Information Service. Minette, lost in pussycat dreams,
curled in her regular spot on the threadbare Persian carpet,
close to the stove that barely glowed despite being stoked
all day.

When Julia tired of memorizing irregular French verbs,
she daydreamed, mostly about food since she was always
hungry. She couldn't stop thinking about that fish lunch in
Rouen. The thought of sole meunière swimming in brown
butter was like Proust's madeleines, releasing a flood of
mouthwatering memories of her first meal in *la belle France* and
the start of her new life.

When the memory grew too tantalizing, she and Paul
would kiss the cat goodnight and head for a neighborhood
bistro, a loud and bustling place that served simple, hearty
fare. Bistro regulars were once assigned a drawer to keep their
napkins, and poodles sat on their own chairs.

Paul and Julia, not yet regulars but well on their way, were
amazed to discover there were five thousand restaurants in
Paris alone. The French practically invented the idea of dining
out and even gave restaurants their name—the first ones served
"fortified" dishes they claimed could restore (*restaurer*) digestive
health. For Julia and Paul the healing power of good food, for
both body and soul, made perfect sense. They began to set

Trois amis

aside Julia's monthly income from a small inheritance for their gustatory adventures.

Paul wrote home that Julia was positively obsessed with tasting sole every place they went, and since the legendary chef Escoffier catalogued 185 ways to prepare it, he figured it might take a while—and a bundle of cash. They would skimp on taxis and cleaning supplies, but never on food for themselves or Minette. With American currency propping up the French economy, one dollar would buy a bistro meal with a small carafe of table wine. A splurge at a temple of cuisine like Maxim's cost a princely sixteen dollars, but the taste sensations—priceless.

Once, while strolling the arcades of the Palais Royal, they came upon a Parisian food shrine, the elegant, two-hundred-year-old Grand Véfour, and couldn't resist. During their meal,

Colette and her chats

they spied a short woman with a bird's nest of hennaed hair, tucked into a banquette at the far end of the dining room. She seemed oblivious to fawning waiters and diners' stares. Their waiter silently mouthed, "Colette"—the grande dame of French letters, now almost eighty. Like the other patrons, they were awestruck. The first woman elected to the venerable Académie française lived in the hotel and, when she didn't dine upstairs with her cats, presided at her regular table.

If she and Julia had a chance to chat, they could have swapped stories about their pussycats. Colette was the most famous "cat lady" in France. In her chorus-girl days, she starred in the pantomime *La chatte amoureuse* in full cat suit, and her wildly popular novel *La chatte* featured her kitty, Saha, as the romantic heroine. It was Colette who once famously pronounced, "There are no ordinary cats." Julia and Paul, already crazy for Minette, totally agreed.

JULIA HAD BECOME a *flâneuse*—a stroller, a saunterer, and (she happily admitted) a loafer. As she soaked up the two-thousand-year-old city's history, art, and culture, she began to see cats everywhere. And no wonder—since Roman times, the City of Light has been a haven for pussycats. In museums and cathedrals, she noticed cats hiding in plain sight—chasing rats in carvings on wooden choir stalls, romping on the pages of richly illuminated prayer books, and adorning the crests of fierce medieval knights.

Cats fired the imagination of writers from Montaigne to Victor Hugo to Cocteau. Some say French cats changed the course of history when they drove the plague-bearing rats from Europe. Parisians have always prized the practical cats that patrol rooftops, elusive cats that lurk in alleyways, beautiful cats that sun themselves on park benches, and regal cats that take their owners out for strolls and stop traffic on the Champs-Élysées. Pussycats accompany Parisians from birth to their final resting place—feral cats still prowl the Père Lachaise Cemetery, comforting mourners and begging for handouts.

Everywhere she went, Julia began to listen for the high-pitched "*Minouminouminouminou*" of housewives calling "Herekittykittykitty"—an invitation to a meal or just a doting pat. The sound triggered a ripple of delight, and she greeted every kitty that crossed her path, especially the black ones, like a long-lost friend. To celebrate their unique je ne sais quoi, she coined a Julia-ism, *poussiequette*, her favorite term of endearment for pussycats from then on.

When her feet gave out after an afternoon window-shopping on the fashionable avenue Montaigne or ducking into tiny galleries in the Marais, she liked to plop down at a sidewalk table among all the tourists, expats, and colorful locals. Every café seemed to have at least one resident pussycat wandering among the marble-topped tables.

Julia's favorite hangout became Café des Deux Magots, at one of the busiest corners on the boulevard Saint-Germain. It was a good place to linger over a *café complet* and study her map, sort out impressions, or just watch the afternoon light fade on the ancient stones of the Church of Saint-Germain-des-Prés across the street.

Everyone there seemed to be Somebody. Janet Flanner, the *New Yorker*'s Paris correspondent, had her own regular table where she nursed a cassis and watched *le tout Paris* pass by. Albert Camus, wreathed in smoke from a stubby Gauloise, often sat scribbling in a back corner, while Paris's power couple, Jean-Paul Sartre and Simone de Beauvoir, preferred the Café de Flore just down the street. Spotting someone famous required a certain Gallic nonchalance that didn't come naturally to the effusive Julia, but she learned to suppress her excitement until she got home and could regale Paul and Minette over an aperitif.

Celebrity spotting was a pastime she shared with columnist Art Buchwald, whom she met at an embassy party. He was in love with Paris too, and so enamored of felines he made his cat the hero of a detective novel. Buchwald gossiped about the characters who filled his "Paris After Dark" column and confided that many famous Parisians were fellow cat people. Camus, for one, doted on his cats, Cali and Gula, and called them "a necessary element" in his life. Paris cats fascinated Chagall too. Floating through several of his paintings is a mysterious cat with a haunting, human face.

Picasso adored his Minou, an elegant Siamese who often posed for him. Because he painted cats so often, some say it's a shame Pablo's oeuvre doesn't include his "Pussycat Period."

Poussiequettes around every corner intensified Julia's passion for all things French. In a letter home, she gushed, "I cannot tell you how much I adore this France and this Paris, these people, their language, their pace, their food, their apartments, their streets. . . . We have found nothing but exquisite friendliness, charm, politeness, warmth, gaiety, downright pleasure. . . . The cats here are, for the most part, big, sleek and wonderful. . . . I am never coming home, so you will just have to come here."

Enchanté, Madame!

ON WEEKENDS, PAUL joined Julia on her sojourns, toting a
tripod and a bag stuffed with a sketchbook, cameras, film, and
filters. Every so often he'd drop to his knees and peer down
a cobbled street to frame a man on a bicycle with a baguette
tucked under his arm, or *chemises* billowing in the breeze from
a balcony.

While Paul studied the scene, Julia studied Paul as he
squinted through his viewfinder. Over time, she began to
see what he saw—the poetry in a curlicued lamppost, a fog-
shrouded steeple, or cats' eyes staring out from shadowy
doorways and lace-curtained windows. Like Julia, he began to
see cats everywhere. As he fiddled with his light meter, she
couldn't resist making friends with his feline subjects. Even the
most skittish tomcat answered her falsetto siren song.

High on the sights and sounds of Paris, Julia and Paul
thought nothing of walking to the far edges of the Right Bank,
through the red-light district of Pigalle, then climbing to the
top of Montmartre for one more glimpse of the city below,
wreathed in the amber glow of sunset. When the light was just
right, they'd scramble to set up his gear before it faded.

Exhausted at the end of a day, they settled into a tiny
bistro where a resident bird chirped in one corner and a fat
white puss lay fast asleep on a pile of ledgers in another. A dog
sporting a green turtleneck sweater watched as two "furiously
animated monkeys ate peanuts . . . filling the place with clatter
and squeals." It struck them both as "wonderfully Parisian."

They set out to explore a new *quartier* almost every week
and kept track of their mission to make the city their own on
a wall map that soon bristled with pushpins marking favorite

spots. Paul's portfolio showcased his growing photo artistry and preferred subjects—his wife, the treelined boulevards of Paris, and pussycats at play or in repose.

LOVE, JUPAULSKI

LETTER-WRITING WAS still a vital art for Parisians, who sent *pneumatiques*, messages stuffed into vacuum tubes that whooshed underground to the nearest *bureau de poste*. Telephones were scarce, service erratic, and calls overseas too expensive. When Roo de Loo finally got a phone, Julia and Paul used it sparingly, preferring their ritual of quietly recording impressions in letters and daybooks, even when the salon was so frosty they had to huddle in bed and write with gloved hands.

Throughout his life Paul craved contact with his twin brother, Charlie, his sounding board and alter ego. He composed an almost daily journal, suffused with wit and intimacy, in an elegant longhand. His nimble mind ranged far and wide—his State Department exhibits, Cold War intrigues and prickly office politics, his search for creative fulfillment, and of course, his Julie, "this darling, sensitive, outgoing, appreciative, characterful & interesting woman."

She preferred to pound her typewriter keys, cramming every inch of the tissue-thin blue airmail paper with single-spaced tales of people they met, food they ate, and the escapades of their new love, Minette: "This pussy of ours is just a darling. I have never seen a cat I liked so much; she gallops all over the house, lies in wait for us, sits in her own chair in the dining room, just loves to be right with us all the time . . . and just couldn't be more fun or nicer."

Letters to Charlie and his wife, Fredericka ("Freddie"), began "Dearest Chafred," an affectionate blend of their two names, and were signed jointly "JuPaul," "JuPaulski," or "Pulia," a symbol of Julia and Paul's deepening bond—two hearts had become one.

When Julia had no time for a letter of her own, she added chatty updates to Paul's wherever she could squeeze in a few lines around the edges of the page, often asking about the animal kingdom in Pennsylvania: "Send more photos of cats & nephews, as well as selves." She complained when no news arrived—"Mimi [Chafred's cat] hasn't written us a word and we are a little hurt"—and she made sure that Minette kept up her end of the correspondence: "Minette wants everyone to know she caught a bird on the roof."

Charlie topped that achievement by claiming that his Mimi was the superior feline because she had invented several cat games. The brotherly competition escalated when Paul bragged that Minette had personally informed him that she—not Mimi—was the gaming genius nonpareil. To prove it, he described her biggest crowd-pleasers, helpfully translating from Minette's native tongue:

- *"Tu te souviens de moi?"* ("Do You Remember Me?") Minette, perched on a dining room chair, bestows a gentle paw pat on the arm of a tablemate every ten seconds to remind them of her undying affection—and appetite.

- *"Où est cette Minou?"* ("Where's the Cat?") When Julie makes the bed, Minette burrows under the sheets and rolls on her back, wriggling and clawing furiously. This game has a championship round, *"J'irai à la blanchisserie"* ("I'm going off to the laundry"). When it's time to gather up the dirty linen, Minette wraps herself in the bedclothes and gets buried in the hamper as JuPaul enact a mock funeral.

- *"La Cavallerie vient au secours!"* ("The Calvary to the Rescue") In a quiet salon, with her roommates absorbed in their books, Minette hides in a corner until they forget all about her. She suddenly streaks through the room, thudding like a herd of buffalo, and vanishes out the opposite door.

- The most challenging game, *"La chute de la nourriture"* ("The Falling Food"), starts with careful selection of *le football*, a small potato from a bag under the kitchen table. Minette noses it to the middle of the floor, stalks it, then pounces and rolls it to the edge of the stairs. With one swat it thump-thump-thumps down to the salon, with Minette scampering after. She retrieves the *ballon* and,

Sisyphus-like, hauls it back up. Multiple rounds ensue. If no *pomme de terre* is available, substitutes may include onions, walnuts, or chicken gizzards.

Paul delivered the coup de grâce when he informed Charlie of a painful truth—Minette, not their Mimi, gave the world *"la Morsure,"* known as "Love Bites," the ultimate kitty pastime.

Julia's high spirits often bubbled onto the page too. She embellished her letters with playful drawings of hearts and arrows and, if Paul was the recipient, lipstick kisses. Though they were rarely apart, when Julia traveled with her father and stepmother to Italy in the spring of 1950, she yearned to return to her Paulski.

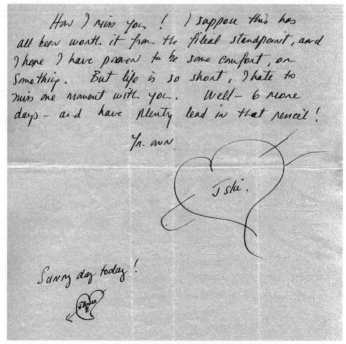

If a letter cried out for an extra-special dose of Julia joie de vivre, she rummaged through her cat stamp collection and squished one onto the paper. A pussycat chasing her tail or curled fast asleep suddenly materialized. To Paul her stamps were "like a bank of organ-stops ready to be interpretively used by Mme l'Artiste. They provide one of the outlets for a quality of Julie's which I particularly cherish." The impish images of pussycats that adorned her letters were a nod to Minette and a sign of the indelible imprint kitties would leave on her heart from now on.

JULIA GOES TO MARKET

JULIA'S LETTERS HOME hinted that her passion for French food had moved beyond the simple act of eating. She sent fewer descriptions of restaurant meals and more ecstatic accounts of her daily trips to local markets. She was beginning to see that a good meal begins with the best ingredients, and to get them you need to make friends in the right places. She later said that discovery changed her life. It certainly improved Minette's.

Marketing meant visiting dozens of shops, each with its own specialty—the *crémerie* for cheese and butter, the *boucherie* for veal chops and venison, the *pâtisserie* for apple tarts and *gâteaux au chocolat*, the charcuterie for country hams and sausage, and of course a stop at the *boulangerie*, often twice a day, for a crusty baguette or *bâtard*, fragrant and warm from the oven. Yesterday's loaves became *pain perdu*, "lost" bread suitable only for stuffing or croutons. If there was no time for the daily trip to les Halles, the sprawling food market in the heart of Paris, open-air produce stalls closer to home offered whatever local farmers picked that morning—tender artichokes, sweet baby peas, or pale pink radishes.

Julia loved feasting her eyes on the shop displays. How perfect to learn that the French call window-shopping *lèche-vitrine* (licking the glass), as if mere looking was like savoring an ice-cream cone. Once inside she could sample to her heart's and tummy's content.

But when she stepped to the counter to buy, some of the jauntiness left her and she became uncharacteristically tongue-tied. Her Smith College French, though rapidly improving, fell short, and she was reduced to pointing and making strange nasal sounds. The vendors weren't impressed.

Even though at six foot two she towered over the petite French housewives, she was awed by the way they muscled their way through the markets, poking, pinching, and squeezing the produce like persnickety government inspectors. Only the very freshest would do. Later she complained to Paul about the pushy matrons with the sharp elbows. He only shrugged—they were just being choosy, and in a country that boasted three hundred cheeses, there was a lot to be choosy about. He encouraged her to be persistent. Once these proprietors got to know her, they'd take to her. He called this gift for winning everyone over "the Juliafication *des gens*."

A fish head was the turning point. One day the market crowds thinned and Julia found herself alone with the fishmonger's wife. She pointed at a filet of sole and the woman nodded curtly, then wrapped it. Julia haltingly asked if there were any fish scraps left. The woman smiled, held up a large fish head, and added it to the package.

The next time Julia came into the shop, the fishwife had set aside another, larger fish head and, with a wink, asked about her pussycat. Julia's French magically improved and the two began exchanging cat tales. Before long, they were gabbing about the fine spring weather, the first salmon of the season, and Julia's plans for cooking her sole. Which wine to go with it. Where to find tender asparagus. Who had the freshest, tastiest pears. And best cheeses. Local gossip. Politics. In-laws. Edith Piaf. Cats who like to go in and out but can't make up their minds. *Enfin*, kisses on both cheeks, two packages of fish in the basket, and fond greetings to Minette. *À bientôt, Madame Child.* Come back soon. Remember the salmon will be in next week. And fish heads for Minette. *Toujours.*

JACKDAW JULIE

JULIA HAD A WEAKNESS for gadgets and loved to hunt for bargains at Dehillerin, a kitchen gear bonanza in les Halles. Paul's salary was stretched thin by the end of the month, so the proprietor was persuaded to let her buy on credit. Her skill at picking through bins of kitchen *junque* reminded Paul of a scavenger bird, so he began calling her "Jackdaw Julie."

Occasionally Julia asked him to join her as she trolled the *marché aux puces*, the giant flea market. The invitation usually meant she had seen just the perfect doohickey, a real steal she couldn't pass up or carry home by herself. One time the object that caught her eye was an enormous marble mortar and pestle Paul described as "big as a baptismal font." He followed her through a dark labyrinth of stalls to reach this treasure, gamely shifted it onto his back, and staggered toward the Blue Flash, breathing hard while Julia chattered about the lovely quenelles she wanted to try, and all the other delights she would soon be grinding, mashing, and pulverizing.

Minette welcomed this latest find after giving it a thorough sniff test. It didn't take long for her to see the potential for quiet naps in the cool, curved marble bowl, especially on warm summer days when ovens were roaring and stockpots bubbling.

Julia's growing collection required new rows of hooks higher up on the wall to hold her acquisitions—a ricer, three sizes of balloon whisks, and a set of measuring cups she had shipped from home after she discovered that the French preferred to add a "handful of this" or a "dollop of that" until the dish tasted just right. Beneath each cup Paul neatly inscribed its size on the wall. Several heavy iron skillets dangled from the lip of the coal stove—irresistible playthings for Minette. She padded on the stovetop, swatted at the dangling spoons, ladles, and saucepans, and set the whole *batterie de cuisine* crazily clanging, a carillon of cookware that brought a halfhearted scold.

The kitchen came with an erratic gadget of its own, meant to compensate for the awkward upstairs/downstairs layout of the apartment. Like waiters who come and go as the spirit moves them, the balky dumbwaiter seemed to deliver meals to the dining room below only when it pleased. In cold weather Minette often dozed inside the contraption, preferring what little warm air might be trapped there to the chilly embrace of the marble mortar.

Julia's lunchtime repertoire was expanding. She found some charming pastry tins and wanted to try her hand at *tartelettes*, the tasty munchies she often snacked on at the market. She lined the little tins with butter and pastry dough, fluted the edges with the back of a knife, pricked the bottoms with a fork, and baked them to a golden brown. The sides collapsed and they weren't as pretty as the ones she bought, but they smelled heavenly. She put them in the dumbwaiter to cool while she whipped up the filling, *fondue de volaille* (chicken in a cream sauce)—one of Paul's favorites.

She sautéed some shallots, brought the cream sauce to a simmer, and finished just as the door slammed below. At that moment a frantic scrabbling came from the back of the dumbwaiter, and before Paul could get up the stairs, Minette shot by him in a blur.

When Julia pulled out the rack of cooling *tartelettes*, every one had been thoroughly tasted and little was left but crumbs. Paul got quite an earful of Julia's growing vocabulary of colorful French expletives, but he soothed her by offering to eat the delicious filling all by itself, as long as it was accompanied by a nice Sauvignon Blanc. They agreed that from now on Julia should always thoroughly check inside the dumbwaiter to be sure a hungry cat wasn't waiting for *le déjeuner*.

THE JOY OF COOKING

WHEN IT CAME to food and cooking, the embassy wives and Julia's friends back home thought she was becoming a bit eccentric. Her curiosity about the flavors in a new dish and her habit of begging the chef for the recipe were seen as odd and slightly déclassé. In the postwar years, American housewives had been led to believe it was shameful to spend so much time in the kitchen. Convenience ruled, with Bisquick, Jell-O, and

Pots, pans, and poussiequette

Gravy Helper lining pantry shelves. Preparing meals for their families was considered a chore, not the joyous experience Julia found in hunting for the freshest ingredients, then peeling, chopping, simmering, and sharing with friends.

Cooking at home in Paris, however, could be a challenge, although she'd finally managed to buy one of the ice-block coolers the French fancifully called *le frigidaire*. Shortages persisted and political unrest brought strikes, so gas and electric service were unpredictable. During one outage, the

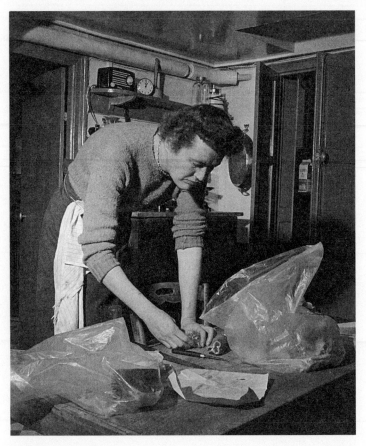

In the Roo de Loo kitchen

iceman didn't cometh, and Julia lamented that several weeks of Minette's frozen dinners had melted.

Through it all, Julia was undaunted. She'd never been happier. She lived in a country obsessed with food, married to a man who adored her and adopted by a cat who made the perfect kitchen companion.

2.

AND KITTY MAKES THREE:
MINETTE MIMOSA
McWILLIAMS CHILD

ALONG WITH HER very own *boulangerie, fromagerie*, and *pâtisserie*, Julia began frequenting the local *vétérinaire*. She noticed Minette rubbing her ear, and after the vet diagnosed a common ear infection, he surprised Julia with the news that their poussiequette, with her three-toned coat, was no ordinary gutter cat but a rare Spanish breed, *le tricolore*. Julia always knew Minette was special: "I never saw another like her . . . her fur is fox-color, black & white in asymmetrical patches like a piece of camouflage for an autumn field." Now Minette was very possibly feline royalty, like the Chartreux, the woolly blue-haired cat with coppery eyes, prized by the French since the Middle Ages.

According to tradition, the Chartreux were bred by the Carthusian monks, who also turned out a high-class, pale green liqueur at a monastery near Grenoble. Charles de Gaulle loved his noble Chartreux cats for their sweet disposition and for being, like the monks, almost mute. Minette, on the other hand, was a feisty kitty with a robust *miaou* and she wasn't afraid to use it. She was more rascally than royal, but that's what tickled Julia and Paul.

They were learning a lot about cats. Minette's ears swiveled like radar at minute sounds that dogs—let alone people—only dream of hearing. Especially the pitter-patter of tiny mouse feet behind baseboards. Feline noses boast an astonishing one hundred million olfactory cells, fourteen times more than humans'. Minette certainly won the cat lottery when she landed in Julia's kitchen, where every day brought heavenly treats for the nose as well as the taste buds. She also had a penchant for plants and flowers, and one day gobbled up a bouquet of mimosas before Jeanne, the maid, could put them in a vase. After that Julia bestowed on Minette a more formal moniker befitting her new elite status: Minette Mimosa McWilliams Child.

One morning Minette wouldn't gobble or even nibble anything and moped listlessly around the apartment. When she refused a bite of her favorite sausage, Julia sensed a real emergency and hustled her to the vet. This time it was something more serious—distemper, or worse, pneumonia. Reluctantly they left her at the clinic for three days. Now it was their turn to mope around the house. After they brought the lethargic kitty home, she took an unexpected turn for the worse. Their poor puss looked half dead, a miserable little fur lump, wheezing under a chair, refusing to budge.

Julia and Paul couldn't bear the thought of losing Minette, so they transformed the salon into a "puss-pital" and nursed her day and night, forcing the kitty to inhale eucalyptus steam and swallow batches of large pills. The gas heater ran constantly until the apartment filled with noxious fumes and they felt queasy too. They didn't even flinch when the vet prescribed kitty suppositories, which worked all too well, forcing them to drape all the chairs with towels.

They had never nursed a sick cat before, let alone one they adored, and all they could do was watch, wring their hands, and fret: "It's sad to see a little animal suffer and not be able to communicate with it."

They had all but given up hope when one miraculous day, without warning, their "one-time-surely-dying pussycat" was up on all fours, looking "lively as a grackle." They both exulted when they saw her green eyes glowing across the dining room table. Minette had reclaimed her usual chair and sat waiting patiently for dinner to be served.

WITH PAUL SETTLED into his new job, Julia was looking for
something useful to *doooo*. To fill an afternoon, she eagerly
accepted an invitation to join some embassy wives for a fashion
show at the House of Dior. She wrote to her sister-in-law,
Freddie, about sitting among rows of women decked out in
sable and diamonds, with "eyes half closed" and a world-weary
look she knew she could never pull off.

Julia was keenly aware of her appearance and had once
flirted with fashion as a career. After college she wrote a style
column for a hometown paper, but her "good cloth coat"
Republican upbringing hadn't prepared her for the fashionistas
who strolled the boulevards of Paris. She was dying to learn
the secrets of those effortlessly chic women. Was it their haute
couture or something more mysterious that made them look
fabulous anywhere, anytime, in anything?

Since the French didn't bother to make dresses for women
her size, she summoned skills she had learned as a Pasadena
debutante-in-training. Upper-middle-class girls like her learned
to apply makeup and took basic cooking and sewing classes
while waiting for Mr. Right to drive up in his new Buick. She
bought stylish patterns to sew her own suits and dresses and
discovered a deep satisfaction in making useful things with her
own capable hands.

Why not make hats too, and maybe even sell them?
Hatmaking had become a trendy hobby among some of her
new embassy friends, so it wasn't hard to find someone to give
her lessons. Soon she was spending afternoons in the drafty
living room, pins between pursed lips, sketching and gluing her
creations. Her market basket was crammed with her new

Playcat

stock-in-trade—feathers, beads, sequins, and tiny birds with sparkly eyes—all of it an answer to a playful cat's prayers.

Minette began each game of "*le chat et le chapeau*" by skidding across Julia's worktable, sending fake bananas and rosebuds flying. Then she'd snatch and hide them all over the apartment. Days later the kitty would suddenly appear with a wild look and a feather in her mouth, then gallop away as if possessed. As expected, Jeanne wouldn't play along, but Julia loved her mischievous cat in the hat.

JULIA WAS FEELING gloomy just thinking about Paul's upcoming trip to Lyon without her. She moaned, "I am a very spoiled woman indeed, because I have hardly at all been separated from my husband even for lunch, and I miss him." But her mood brightened when her sister, Dorothy, arrived for an extended stay *chez Child*.

"Dort" was a younger, even taller McWilliams, with a voice eerily similar to Julia's. She breezed into Roo de Loo like a springtime zephyr, gushing about her Atlantic crossing and the *marrrrrvelous* people she collected along the way—an old English baron, a charming French widow, an actress, and her dubious companion, the *Roué*. She helpfully impersonated all of them for her bemused hosts in fractured but enthusiastic French.

Lured by the sisters' swooping laughter, Minette came to join the party with a battered brussels sprout in her mouth. Once she had their attention, she dropped it on the carpet and swatted it under the sofa. Dort got down on all fours, reached into the dust bunnies, grabbed the sprout, and bounced it back to Minette. They pitched it back and forth until nothing remained but a pile of leaves and a panting pussycat. A new *compagnon* was in the house.

JuPaul agreed that Dort's first Parisian experience should be a sublime meal. They chose a small neighborhood restaurant on the rue Montorgueil that came with Julia's highest endorsement: "the best food I've had (they REALLY CARE)." The next day they took the "standard JuPaulski Walk #1" around their Saint-Germain-des-Prés neighborhood, ending with drinks at their favorite café, Deux Magots, or in Julia parlance, "two maggots." Julia proudly took Dort around to meet the butcher, the fishmonger, and her new best friend, Marie des Quatre-Saisons. The rosy-cheeked blonde, who ran a tiny *crémerie* just around the corner, could judge the ripeness of her cheeses to the hour, or so it seemed to Julia.

The two sisters spent a luscious afternoon ambling arm in arm through the Luxembourg Gardens, munching on waffles and fresh raspberry juice from a sidewalk cart. It was Easter vacation, and the park was full of children tugging on balloons and nannies pushing prams. They watched the children play while catching up on family gossip and each other's lives. Although Julia and Dort looked and sounded so much alike, they had scarcely spent any time together as adults, and relished this chance to become reacquainted. Through her sister's eyes, Julia was falling in love with the City of Light all over again.

When Dort got around to unpacking her trunk, she discovered she had a helper. Telltale bits of chewed paper lay scattered all around, and she found a small potato buried under a pile of sweaters—Minette's calling card. The cat had pawed her lingerie into a tangle and sat smugly inside one of Dort's spacious shoes with a brassiere draped rakishly over one ear. It was clear to Julia the mischievous Minette was well on the way to "making Dortie's life HELL."

One day Julia and Dort were practicing how to be French on the telephone. Dort held her nose and chirped loudly: *"OUI, OUI, J'ÉCOUTE!"* (Yes, yes, I hear you!) Minette, who was sleeping in a flowerpot, sat bolt upright. Her ears stiffened, and she leaped onto Dort's lap and nipped her hand. Next it was Julia's turn. She pinched her nose and squeaked, *"Oui, oui, j'écoute!"* and she too was rewarded with a little love bite.

Again and again the sisters emitted nasally shrieks, and

each time Minette answered with a friendly nip. Dort thought
they had trained the cat to perform a unique trick, but Julia
guessed that their high-pitched voices must have been touching
"some chord of amorous response." It was springtime, after all,
and Minette was a frisky *jeune fille*.

MATCHMAKING IS NO *PIQUE-NIQUE*

WARM BREEZES WAFTING through the windows of Roo de
Loo lifted the spirits of every resident, including Minette,
who had a serious case of *printemps* fever. She raced up and
down the stairs at breakneck speed, tumbled into laps for an
instant, then flew to the door and yowled pitifully. Julia and Paul
thought it just might be a young kitty's fancy turning to love.

They felt their own springtime urges. Hand in hand they
took long strolls along the Seine, and every warm weekend
they piled into the Blue Flash and headed out to explore the
countryside, often with friends. One bright April day, Julia
decided to throw together a last-minute picnic to celebrate the
oceans of red tulips blooming in the parks. She made an early
market run to fill a basket with the makings of a simple but
tasty lunch: crisp baguettes with sweet Normandy butter, cold
tarragon chicken, *salade verte vinaigrette, fromages*, fruits, and of
course, vin du pays. Plenty of vin du pays.

The bois de Boulogne was a favorite *pique-nique* spot,
especially after Paul pointed out that the Impressionist Édouard
Manet chose this leafy glade as the setting for his masterpiece,
Le déjeuner sur l'herbe (Luncheon on the grass). The idea of
picnicking in the nude like the woman in the painting
appealed to Paul, but Julia demurred. The weather could be
so changeable.

Spring fever

So it was on this day when they planned to dine alfresco with their French friends, Jean Asche and his wife, Thérèse. As the hour drew near, the skies suddenly turned dark, wet, and windy, ruling out a blanket in the park. Undeterred, Julia suggested they picnic at Roo de Loo.

The couple arrived with a surprise in their picnic basket: a macho white tomcat with tiger markings and an eye for *les femmes*. For some time there had been talk of Maquis as a potential suitor for Minette, and the indoor picnic was a perfect chance to test the chemistry. According to letters written by their surrogates, Jean and Julia, "Maquis and Minette have been exchanging loving messages for a year."

The moment the guests set down their hamper, Minette's radar detected a gentleman caller. She hurtled down the stairs into the salon and screeched to a halt as Jean raised the lid. Maquis stepped boldly from the basket and locked eyes with Minette. Love at first sight it was not. The tomcat flattened against the floor, his tail puffed up three times its normal size, twitching and snapping.

Minette assumed a similar defensive crouch, but welcomed the intriguing guest with short little burping noises. Her come-hither tones were lost on Maquis, who snarled as he inched backward toward his basket. Like Julia, Minette was a stranger to rejection, so she redoubled her flirtatious purrs—*ronron, ronron*—but that only made Maquis more desperate to disappear.

The standoff lasted more than four hours while the picnickers ate their way through the basket of delights. Occasionally they heard the star-crossed lovers *miaou*ing as they moved from the salon to the kitchen to—momentarily promising—the *chambre à coucher*, but the magic never materialized. Every so often Julia took a peek, but it was clear the romance was a nonstarter.

Not a moment too soon for the exhausted Maquis, Jean returned him to his hamper, his macho reputation in tatters. *Au revoir. À bientôt.* For a while, Minette rubbed against the closed door but soon ambled off to nose around the leftovers. Like any spurned lover, she would eat her way out of a broken heart by finishing off a bowl of *crème anglaise.*

A SWELLEGANT, ELEGANT PARTY

LIKE HER SISTER, Dort was a people person, so it didn't take long to find a community of simpatico friends, mostly expats living a version of *la vie de bohème* on the Left Bank. She found an unpaid job at the American Club Theater, and soon a parade of actors, writers, scene painters, puppeteers, and musicians was hanging out at Roo de Loo, where food, wine, and conversation flowed freely. She began keeping steady company with Ivan Cousins, who, like Paul, was everything her straitlaced Republican father was not. A free-spirited aspiring actor who once took classes with Gregory Peck, he too fell under the spell of the infectious McWilliams joie de vivre. Also like Paul, Ivan was a foot shorter than his sweetheart.

Julia was delighted by Dort's knack for filling the house with offbeat characters, and the stepped-up social whirl. Paul not so much. He preferred small dinner parties for close friends and was happiest spending an evening with his two *femmes,* Julia and Minette. But even he applauded Julia's plan to throw an ambitious party for the wedding of their friend Hadley Mowrer's son. Captain Jack Hemingway lived in Berlin and his bride in Idaho—why not get married in Paris? The Mowrers asked Julia to be the matron of honor because she was the only friend they had in Paris who was taller than the bride.

Julia didn't care. She was thrilled, not only to be in the wedding party—in a suit and hat she made herself—but to show off her growing culinary skills. She envisioned a star-studded guest list—the groom's father, Ernest Hemingway, might even show up. Dort was awestruck watching her sister whisk egg whites into submission and expertly flatten chicken breasts with her wooden cudgel. She had never seen such a gaggle of gadgets growing up. Their mother, Caro, mainly visited the kitchen on the cook's night off to fix one of her specialties—baking powder biscuits, Welsh rarebit, and codfish balls—or to supervise the children making melted cheese sandwiches.

But *ooh la la*—just look at Julia now! The sisters chortled, picturing their father's face when he learned that his Smith College–educated debutante daughter had found her bliss. As a cook! A French cook at that. He dismissed the French as fainthearted snail-eaters.

Among the terrines, pâtés, and mousselines—some store-bought, some homemade—that jammed the sideboard was Julia's pièce de résistance, a whole sea bass in quivering gelée. Thumbing through *Larousse Gastronomique*, she saw an elaborately decorated fish that seemed just the thing to impress arty guests. After studying the photos, she used an edible palette of carrots, watercress, tomatoes, capers, and mayonnaise to "paint" scales, fins, and other piscine details on her fish canvas. After a few sips of cooking wine, she let her imagination take flight, and when she was done, her bass sported a sly grin and one squinty eye. She judged it to be amusing, though not quite ready for *Larousse*.

As twilight fell on Roo de Loo, the soft glow of candlelight magically transformed the shabby-chic salon. The worn sofa and chairs were pushed against the wall, the faded satin draperies pulled back, and the windows thrown open to the perfumed air of a perfect June evening. It was almost party time, and Minette, who was interested in the fanciful fish but didn't like crowds, scampered off at the first clang of the elevator cage.

The room soon filled with some faces Dort had only seen in magazines—friends of the Mowrers and Paul's old chums from the twenties. Julia was especially thrilled to meet a tiny woman in a floppy-brimmed hat who held court in a corner of the room between frequent trips to the buffet. The exotic, birdlike creature with the hearty appetite was none other than Alice B. Toklas—she and Gertrude Stein were the groom's godparents. As the evening wore on, heads swiveled when each new guest arrived, the room abuzz that Papa Hemingway himself might appear and expound on his latest novel or the exploits of the six-toed cats he doted on at his Havana home.

The buffet table looked as though a famished army, not a band of picky guests, had descended, leaving only fish bones and a few tired parsley sprigs. The reluctantly departing partyers showered Julia with a litany of favorite dishes and compliments to the chef. Her first big society affair was a whopping success.

When the front door closed for the last time, Julia surveyed the mountain of dirty dishes and cursed her failure to properly train the cat. By now Minette, like all good daughters, should have been willing to help with kitchen cleanup. But alas, it was too late to teach this cat new tricks. Minette's idea of "helping" was to lick eggs or fish off plates. Julia lamented, "I must have brought her up wrong."

WHILE JULIA WAS browsing through *Le Monde* with Minette
one lazy Saturday morning, a photo of a cat sporting a chic
chapeau caught her eye. Le Cat Club de Paris was holding its
annual show. Who could resist? So later that afternoon JuPaul
found their way to le Continental, an ornate fin de siècle hotel
with a gilded banquet hall full of *miaou*ing cats. Beneath a
gigantic crystal chandelier, dozens of large cages festooned
with paper streamers, flowers, and flags lined the room.

Julia and Paul strolled from cage to cage peering at the
diminutive decor. Lucky kitties lounged on overstuffed sofas
or reclined on stacks of pink satin pillows, and a few indolently
batted feathery toys and stuffed mice across the tiny carpets.
Fastidious felines, and the occasional human, preened in the
mini mirrors on cage walls. Exhibitors who were sticklers for
detail matched the furnishings to their breed—pampered
Persians snoozed on oriental rugs, while sleek Siamese ate fresh
sole from lotus-themed china.

Some cages attracted passersby with flirtatious notes:
"*Je m'appelle Nitou et je suis très gentille.*" ("My name is Nitou and
I'm very sweet.") Julia was easily seduced. Eyes dancing, she
rushed up to each kitty condo, wiggled her fingers through the
mesh, and crooned endearments. Some doting owners even let
her cuddle their prized pussies. More than once Paul had to
persuade her to give the kitty back, step away from the cage,
and move on. As the cat fanciers beamed, Julia blew kisses and
trilled "*Bonne chance*" to her new fuzzy friends. Her ebullience
was contagious, in any language.

Paul had witnessed this "Julia effect" many times before
and could see it coming. "Those curious, green orbs develop a

phosphorescent sparkle and that mobile mug takes on a look of pleasurable anticipation and the first thing you know, she's imbued the atmosphere with her own aurora-borealis."

The flamboyant exhibitors were as fascinating and eccentric as their pets. They gossiped about the competition, shared tips on coping with finicky eaters, and whispered surefire hair-ball cures. As the afternoon wore on, Paul's tolerance for extreme cat-centricity reached its limit when he noticed one kitty whose owner had fitted him with a pair of green cat's-eye sunglasses. The pussycat in shades was curled up beside a coffee table with a box of tiny cigarettes and an ashtray. Another wore pink silk booties. Paul grumpily chalked it up to frustrated motherhood, but Julia got a kick out of the over-the-top spectacle.

As Paul was the first to admit, his own disposition was not nearly as sunny or forgiving as Julia's. More prone to melancholy, he ruminated to his brother that their personality differences were real but never a source of conflict. He knew he got the best of the bargain: "I hate to think what . . . I might have been without that face to look at."

That afternoon, Julia's face was beaming. She was happy to be in the company of so many kindred spirits who were unashamed to publicly adore cats. Attending cat shows became one of her favorite outings wherever she happened to be. Julia Child was now a cat lady and proud of it.

3.

MASTERING THE ART OF FRENCH COOKING

WHEN THE ALARM went off at six thirty on a chilly October morning, Julia wondered what she had gotten herself into. Still snozzling from a nasty cold, she kicked off the covers, dumping Minette onto the floor. The rudely awakened cat trotted up to the kitchen but would have to wait for Paul to get her breakfast, since Julia barely had time to gulp down a glass of tomato juice before dashing off. By the time she revved the Blue Flash, her jitters had vanished and she brimmed with excitement.

She was on her way to le Cordon Bleu, said to be the best culinary school in the world, to learn everything she could about French cooking. Urged on by friends who swooned over her dinners and with a notion to open a restaurant one day with her *belle-soeur*, Freddie, she needed more formal training. All they had now was a name, "Mrs. Child's and Mrs. Child's." What they lacked was know-how. Paul's enthusiasm for the project was fueled by self-interest: Behind their wives' restaurant, he imagined he and Charlie would eat like princes, throwing parties for all their friends.

That first morning Julia had no illusions—she would roll up her sleeves and prove she could keep up with the chefs-in-training. She had struggled to convince the school's director, the sour Madame Brassart, that she belonged in the yearlong course with the serious students, not the six-week course for housewives, and she gladly plunked down "450 smackers." She discovered that the "serious" students were eleven former army cooks studying on the GI Bill, with ambitions to take over a family bakery in Nebraska or a pizza parlor in New Jersey. She quickly sized them up: nice guys, but not an artist among them. She'd been around army bases during the war and wasn't intimidated by this all-male group, but Paul gleefully noted that "the boys are bravely trying to get used to the idea that their masculine club has been invaded by a dame."

Class met from seven fifteen to nine thirty every morning in a narrow basement kitchen with two long cutting tables and three gas stoves running down the middle, with electric ovens and an icebox at either end. Julia didn't inspect the facilities too closely—there were rumors about the school's spotty hygiene, and as time went on she was sure they could use Minette's discreet mouse relocation services.

Students could lunch on what they made that morning, but she ran home to cook for Paul and amuse the pussycat, who pined for her playmate. At two thirty, it was back to school for the chef presentations in a large upstairs classroom with banked seats: "Just like a hospital where the interns sit up in a Roman amphitheatre & the surgeon (a visiting chef) demonstrates how to amputate a leg (make a cream sauce)."

She instantly liked the seventy-year-old Chef Bugnard, who once studied under the great Escoffier. His informal style suited her: "It's a free-for-all thing and you got to keep your ears open and ask what you want." As they sliced, chopped, and stirred, Bugnard called out measurements in rat-a-tat French and regaled them with inside stories about recipes and the famous chefs who created them.

Julia thanked her lucky stars, and Berlitz, for her fluency in French, and even more for the long hours tending her own stove. She felt supremely ready for this new challenge and, after only a week, crowed, "I have noticed the most TREMENDOUS difference already in my cooking. . . . How terrible and *funeraille* [deadly] if we had a cook!"

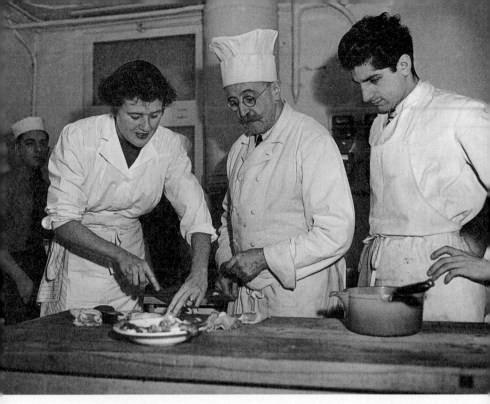

Practice makes parfait

Her aspirations were already clear. In homage to the great French gourmand Brillat-Savarin, she signed one of her letters home "J. Brillat-Child."

PAW DE DEUX

THE FIRST DAY at le Cordon Bleu went by in a blur, and as soon as the afternoon demonstration ended, Julia strode out onto the rue du Faubourg Saint-Honoré with a shopping list in hand. Tonight's dinner for Paul, Dort, and Minette would reprise *pigeons rôtis délicieux*—tender little birds stuffed and skewered just the way Chef Bugnard did them in class. *La chasse* (hunting season) was in full swing, and shop windows were strung with game. She discovered that the French, and their pussycats, were happy to find birds of every feather roasted, stewed, fried, and fricasseed on their dinner plates.

Julia got to work plucking the pigeons, tucking bits of butter under the skin, and carefully threading them onto skewers. Like Julia, Minette was in constant motion, pirouetting from sink to stove and back again, leaping for tidbits that fell from Julia's hands. It was a kind of *coup de ballet parisien*, as French chefs call their habit of scooping up food that falls on the floor and, with a shrug, tossing it back into the pot. In Julia and Minette's own "paw de deux," nothing edible ever hit the floor.

When the pigeons were done, Julia arranged them on the platter, feet daintily tucked under. The cranky dumbwaiter had decided to take the night off, so she had to carry everything down to the dining room herself. But the presentation of her first Cordon Bleu meal for Paul and Dort cried out for something special, a touch of drama perhaps. Julia raised the platter aloft and nodded to Minette, who hadn't taken her eyes off the juicy birds all afternoon. The cat didn't need to be asked twice—she sprang onto Julia's shoulder and draped herself around her neck like a live boa. The pair triumphantly descended the staircase to a thrilled chorus of *ooh la la*s.

To Paul and Dort's delight, Julia diligently did her homework every night, and they gladly devoured it, but Paul felt a bit like a "kitchen widower." If he wanted to be near his wife, he had to sit in the kitchen and watch her practice pulling the guts out of a chicken through a tiny hole in its neck or removing all the bones from a goose without tearing the skin.

The sight of Julia in her blue denim apron, with a wooden

spoon in each hand, and Minette leaping for scraps reminded him less of a balletic pas de deux than a symphony, with Julia as the kettle-drummer: "The oven door opens & shuts so fast you hardly notice the deft thrust of a spoon as she dips into a casserole & up to her mouth for a taste-check like a perfectly-timed double-beat on the drums. She stands there surrounded by a battery of instruments with an air of authority & confidence."

In just a few months, Julia was sure she had entered a whole new world: "I feel it in my hands, my stomach, my soul. There is so much to learn, so much to practice. I feel I have my foot in the door and am beginning 'to see,' but I have such a long way to go."

Paul's hit parade of dishes included *coquilles Saint Jacques, canard à l'orange, crème Chantilly, galantine de volaille*, and *soufflé Grand Marnier*. Although he didn't regret a single bite, he was clearly losing the battle of the belt. Since Julia started at le Cordon Bleu, he had been forced to add three more notches and was flirting with a full-blown *crise de foie*, the tummy trouble everyone called "American stomach in Paris." Dort's belts seemed to be getting tighter too. Minette, however, wasn't worried—everyone knows that French cats don't get fat.

CORDON BLUES

JULIA HAD FOUND her bliss. After six months at le Cordon Bleu, she knew twenty ways to cook fish and could bone a duck in her sleep. She finally had a focus for her life, but her mind wandered as she watched Chef Bugnard whip up yet another baba au rhum, and she dozed off when he prepared sole *à la normande* for the fourth time. More sleep was beginning to sound good after so many mornings up at six and practicing in her own kitchen often past midnight.

It was time to move on. Paul's job would keep them overseas for a while, so that restaurant dream with Freddie was on hold. But Julia was hatching another plan—a cooking school for Americans in Paris. Her school would offer students something Madame Brassart's exalted *école* could never deliver—friendly, supportive instruction along with a passionate appreciation for food.

At le Cercle des Gourmettes, a ladies' eating club, she met two lively Frenchwomen, Louisette Bertholle and Simone "Simca" Beck, expert cooks with food always on their minds. The three hit it off and in an instant, the faculty of *l'École des trois gourmandes*, "The School of the Three Hearty Eaters," was in place. Only one thing was missing: a piece of parchment bearing a Maltese cross on a blue sash, Julia's official diploma from le Cordon Bleu, to hang on the wall of her kitchen classroom.

To get it, all she had to do was pass the final exam, but her nemesis Madame Brassart was stalling. She still fumed over Julia's insistence on taking the course for professional cooks rather than the one for "fluffies," and for months ignored Julia's pleas to schedule her test. She relented only when she got a subtly threatening letter on US Embassy stationery, hinting that word might get around about the school's mistreatment of American students, especially the many GIs whose regular government checks kept it in business. Elated, Julia rehearsed some of the more challenging recipes she'd mastered: *filet de sole Walewska, poularde à la toulousaine, sauce vénitienne*. She couldn't wait to strut her stuff. *Allons-y!*

On test day Julia's pen flew across the page of the written

exam. She confidently handed Madame her paper and followed her down the hall to the demonstration kitchen for part two. When she read the directions, she stopped smiling. The wily one had set a trap: cook three servings of *œufs mollets* with béarnaise sauce, *côtelettes de veau en surprise*, and *crème renversée au caramel*. Julia couldn't believe her eyes. This was a menu for beginners, not for serious students like herself who expected, even welcomed, a rigorous test of culinary prowess.

She dimly recalled seeing these recipes in the little pamphlet she was handed on her first day but never bothered to look at again. She decided to improvise, but the results didn't amuse Madame Brassart, who swiftly delivered the fatal blow—a failing grade. Her pronouncement that Mrs. Child did "not have any great natural talent for cooking" would be remembered as the most colossal misjudgment in culinary history. Julia later dismissed this verdict with a withering riposte: "Mrs. Brassart is Belgian, not French."

Furious with herself for failing the simple test, Julia stormed down to the basement kitchen alone and cooked the menu again, flawlessly. She never doubted her abilities, and neither did those who mattered most—her mentor Chef Bugnard, Paul, and anyone who had the good fortune to eat at Roo de Loo. Shortly after the debacle, Bugnard persuaded Madame Brassart to let him be the judge of a retest in Julia's own kitchen.

The timing was perfect. She and Paul had recently given the place a face-lift and added three square-top stools so they could now seat seven people, or six people and one cat, "if we don't have to be formal about it." The finishing touch was the coveted blue ribbon in its handsome frame, proof that Mrs. Child had mastered the art of French cooking.

Reserved seat

THE SCHOOL OF
THE THREE HEARTY EATERS

ON THE FIRST day of class at her fledgling school, Julia's kitchen suddenly seemed cramped. How would it hold two more *profs*, three American-sized students, and Minette, who refused to give up her personal stool? They originally planned to hold class in Louisette's spacious kitchen, but her remodel wasn't ready. Neither were the three would-be teachers when Julia got a call from an old California friend who saw their ad for cooking lessons in the embassy newsletter. This friend had rounded up two companions and wouldn't take no for an answer, so ready or not, the School of the Three Hearty Eaters was open for business.

The faculty arrived, market baskets brimming with leeks, potatoes, apples, and sweet Normandy butter. They quickly organized their tools, sharpened knives, and donned aprons. Pinned to each crisp white smock was the logo Paul designed, *l'École des trois gourmandes* in script encircling a large curlicued *3* that looked a little like a corkscrew.

Promptly at 10 AM, the novices crowded into the kitchen, all hats, gloves, and stylish suits as if they were going to a Junior League luncheon in Pasadena. Julia handed them aprons and collected six hundred francs each—about two dollars a lesson, including lunch.

Supersized Julia stood next to the merely tall five-foot-ten Simca, who was beside the petite and *très chic* Louisette. Simca was a whiz at technique and delivered firm opinions about everything in heavily accented English. The charming Louisette was fluent in English but a bit cavalier when it came to organization. To Julia, her colleagues' most valuable asset was a lifetime in France.

The two Frenchwomen were trying to publish a cookbook for Americans, but without much luck. Julia wasn't surprised. Their book was a random collection of recipes that home cooks would find impossibly daunting. Where on earth would Americans find fresh ox blood? Certainly not the A&P. Julia knew where housewives in the States were coming from—

supermarkets full of frozen fish sticks, Betty Crocker cake mixes, and orange bricks of Velveeta. Their kitchens boasted Amana freezers and Waring blenders—machines designed to save time and get them out of the kitchen.

Julia called the class to order and made introductions, including Minette Mimosa McWilliams Child, placidly perched on her stool. As the slicing, dicing, and whisking accelerated, Minette scanned the floor beneath the table for bits of dough, puddles of cream, and the occasional broken egg yolk. If anything edible hit the floor, Minette discreetly slipped down, tidied up, and returned to her roost.

The kitty added to the ambience, which was exactly what Julia had hoped it would be: "homey and fun and informal, and passionate pleasure from both pupils and *professeurs*." Everyone felt at ease, free to admit mistakes and learn from them. But errors were few and Julia felt a little guilty that Minette wasn't getting her fair share of the feast.

The first menu: *potage Parmentier*, leek and potato soup, a mainstay of every French home cook, and *tarte normande aux pommes*, classic custard-apple tart, a specialty of Simca's Normandy. The morning flew by in an aromatic cloud of simmering stock mingled with sweet pastry tart, cinnamony apples, and friendly chatter. When it was time to finish the soup, Julia poured in a generous dollop of heavy cream just as the glistening dessert tarts emerged from the oven to rapturous sighs.

Julia turned to give the soup a final stir and found herself staring at a coagulated mess. Woe! While admiring the novice cooks' triumphs, she forgot to take the pot off the heat. Now the once creamy blend of pureed potatoes, leeks, and broth had separated into a lumpy, watery brew the color of fresh

Teachers' pet

cement. Simca clucked and began to apologize, but Julia cut
her off. *Oui!* She had made a mistake, but there was a good
lesson to be learned. Adding cream to boiling broth will make
it curdle. She knew that, of course. The soup wasn't pretty but
even so it would taste quite *marrrrrvelous*. The students dipped
their spoons into the unpromising mix, and voilà! As predicted,
the soup tasted just fine. In fact, *délicieuse!*

Appointing himself visiting professor of oenology, Paul
joined the ladies for lunch. He poured the wine generously,

making the already high-spirited gathering feel like a party. As they ate, Julia used the curdled soup to give another bit of sage advice: "Never apologize." That only draws attention to the meal's shortcomings and guests start to feel bad for the cook. "Maybe the cat has fallen into the stew . . . *eh bien, tant pis!*" At that, the ladies glanced around nervously for Minette. Her stool was empty, but the hungry cat had merely moved to her usual lunch spot on Paul's lap. Looking relieved, they polished off their soup and lingered over another glass of wine.

COOKERY BOOKERY

WORD GOT AROUND fast. *L'École des trois gourmandes* was the in place if you wanted to learn French cooking. The trio of teachers made the classes fun, and where else would you have a cat for a classmate? Encouragement flowed freely, but beneath the casual charm was discipline, expertise, and passion that appealed to women like Julia herself, curious and serious about the world of food.

Their school's success breathed fresh life into the idea of a French cookbook for Americans. Simca and Louisette's slim spiral-bound book, *What's Cooking in France*, had sold poorly. Undeterred, they submitted six hundred more pages to their New York publisher, but Putnam found the bigger manuscript vague and frustrating and refused to greenlight the project unless they got an American collaborator.

Professeur Julia agreed to get involved if her partners were willing to start over. She had a plan for a teaching manual, not just a recipe book, along with a new title: *French Home Cooking*. Julia saw the book as an extension of her classroom: thorough, practical, and fun. Above all, it would be easy to follow—as if Julia were at the cook's elbow offering help and encouragement.

Before she wrote a word, she tested and tasted relentlessly. In one day, she made *soupe aux choux* (cabbage soup) using three different methods. Paul patiently evaluated them all, but Minette turned up her nose, especially at the batch made with a pressure cooker, the latest laborsaving device from back home. Julia agreed with the cat and banished the clunky, hissing pot to the "forgettery."

Paul and Minette kept Julia company as she bustled around the kitchen. He read aloud from their favorite books, like Boswell's *London Journal*, which Julia found almost as fascinating as her own Paulski's diaries. When she blithely predicted she'd finish the cookbook in six months, Paul saw the timeline stretching into the future, to the end of Boswell and possibly through the complete works of Balzac. He knew adapting French culinary technique for American kitchens would be a monumental job, and the burden would fall to his capable but overly optimistic wife.

Julia finished the first chapter, on sauces, in December 1952, sent it off to New York, and held her breath. She went back to working on the soup chapter, but at the end of January, Putnam rejected the whole approach as much too ambitious. Julia and her partners vowed to push on and find a more sympathetic publisher. Meanwhile, Julia's Boston pen pal, Avis DeVoto, had fallen in love with the manuscript and sent it to her publishing connections. Soon the *trois gourmandes* were toasting a new offer with flutes of bubbly.

But their high spirits dissipated faster than the champagne fizz. Change had been hanging in the air at Roo de Loo for several months. Paul had overstayed his Paris posting, and relocation rumors were growing louder by the day. Where would they end up? Bonn? Norway? London? Back in the States?

Julia, a graduate of the most prestigious cooking school in Paris and an accomplished teacher deep into "cookery bookery," faced her uncertain future in typical fashion—she worked even harder. Hunched over her Underwood, she churned out single-spaced onionskin pages with five carbon copies and stacked the growing pile neatly next to the stove.

While Julia typed like a mad woodpecker, Paul kept a grip on normal by sketching scenes of the Paris he loved, views out their windows and their playful poussiequette. But Minette wouldn't sit still for her portrait—she too felt the vibes of their shifting fortunes. "Oh, for a crystal ball! Where will we be in six months? What doing? It seems unlikely that we'll be drawing Paris rooftops and writing Cookbooks."

IN JANUARY 1953, the Childs' crystal ball revealed boats bobbing in the sun and bowls of fish stew. Paul had been named Cultural Affairs Officer for the southern part of France, based at the American consulate in Marseille. After four and a half glorious years, they had to say good-bye to their beloved Paris, but at least they'd be staying in *la belle France*.

JuPaul left the cold, rainy streets of Paris behind to scout out their new city. Paul loved the tempo of the raucous old port: "There seems to be 10 times as much horn-blowing, gear-clashing, shouting, whistling, door-banging, dropping of lumber, breaking of glass, blaring of radios, boat-whistling, gong-clanging, brake-screeching, angry shouting as anywhere else." Julia took to the boldly seasoned, fish-centric Mediterranean diet, washed down with muscular young regional wines. And the bouillabaisse! The timing of this move couldn't have been better, since she was about to start the fish chapter of her cookery book.

Leaving their beloved Roo de Loo was sure to be traumatic. Julia wondered how they ever saw the charm in these rooms four years ago, when they were chock-full of "floozy superfloo," Madame Perrier's faded belle époque decor. But now this home was where their hearts would always be, and they couldn't imagine feeling the same about any other place. Julia even wrote to Charlie and Freddie, suggesting they consider renting it to keep the apartment in the family, a Parisian pied-à-terre, a steal at $140 a month including electricity, though that still worked fitfully.

For Julia, it was doubly hard to bid adieu to her colleagues, who reluctantly decided to carry on with the cooking school in Louisette's big blue kitchen. She planned to return as often as possible to work on the cookbook. In the meantime, she would keep her Underwood hopping and *la poste* in business sending packages of neatly typed pages zipping to Paris, Marseille, and their agent in Boston.

Between packing and farewell parties, Julia and Paul made tearful rounds of their favorite haunts. They grieved for the loss of Paris as if it were a loved one, passing through the stages of denial, resignation, and finally acceptance: "Paris won't be the same with us gone. . . . No other city will ever seem so wonderful for us ex-Parisians. . . . Our hearts have been infected, and will always skip a beat at the mention of our city."

They left the most painful parting for last. Julia wrote: "We are regretfully having to leave our darling Minette Mimosa McWilliams Child in Paris . . . as our life in Marseille, until we find an adequate living establishment, cannot take a pussy. It's like wrenching off one's left breast."

On her farewell tour of favorite shops, she poured out her sadness at having to leave Minette. Maria, her vegetable seller and one of her favorite Parisian women, had an idea. She knew that the old woman who owned the charcuterie had recently lost her own kitty to old age and was inconsolable. Maybe she could keep Minette company until Julia's life in Marseille settled down. Julia talked it over with Paul, then tucked Minette into a hamper and went to pay a call. She had to make sure the match was right, but she needn't have worried. The woman's eyes lit up when she met the frisky, affectionate poussiequette Julia had talked so much about. It was a reprise of that moment four years earlier when Minette leaped out of a market basket and into Julia's heart. The union was sealed when madame offered her new companion a scoop of her special reserve *pâté de maison*.

And there was more where that came from. Much more. Madame lived above her shop, a cornucopia of charcuterie, with a window draped in skinny breakfast *saucisses* and fat smoked *saucissons* and display cases jammed with *pâté en croûte* and *pâté de campagne*, pork terrines, hams, and *confit d'oie* (preserved goose). Madame had a toasty kitchen and a friendly old dog for company. Julia knew Minette would be happy there as *la chatte de la charcutière*. The second of her nine lives, like the first, would be filled with love and tasty delights.

Au revoir, mon amie

JULIA TOO HAD new lives ahead of her—best-selling author, teacher, TV star, and culinary icon. From Paris, Julia and Paul's travels took them to Marseille, Germany, Washington, D.C., Norway, and, after Paul retired from the Foreign Service, a permanent home in Cambridge, Massachusetts. Through all the moves and years, the loves of her life remained constant.

Paul, of course. During one of their rare separations, she wrote, "Life is a dull thud, an onionless sauce, a nothing-at-all without you." And he thought he was the luckiest man alive: "Julie . . . looks younger, more beautiful & ageless than ever. . . . I am continuously happy & satisfied to be married to her & I hope it lasts forever."

Pussycats. Before Paris, Julia admitted that she had never really known cats, but "since Minette and other French cats, I just love pussies." In the decade after Paris, Paul's job meant they were always being uprooted, so she couldn't have a cat to call her own, but every time she saw one, she fell under the old spell. Alley cats and strays or the feline friends of friends—she couldn't resist scooping them up and giving a squeeze. Each one reminded her of Minette and those magical days at Roo de Loo.

La belle France. It would always be their North Star, and hardly a day went by that Julia and Paul didn't feel it beckoning, "when we hear chimes at midnight, or taste a Pouilly-Fumé, or hear somewhere a snatch of that low-brow tonk-a-tonk music that's so typically French." Or hear the plaintive *miaou*ing of a poussiequette choir.

The Book would bring them back to France. After ten long years, *Mastering the Art of French Cooking* was finally published by Alfred A. Knopf in 1961, and Julia became an "overnight sensation."

4.

RETURN TO PARADISE:
A HOUSE IN PROVENCE

La Pitchoune

"THE LITTLE THING"

THE SEA DANCED in the rearview mirror and palm trees
waved a welcome as the rented Peugeot headed inland. It
lurched through hairpin turns, swooped down a final hill, then
up a dusty drive toward a construction site. Julia let out a
whoop when she saw the half-finished stucco house perched on
the hill. La Pitchoune, "the little thing," was the dream that got
them through some dark days and cold nights in Plittersdorf,

near Bonn, and Oslo. Since leaving France in 1954, they had fantasized about a place of their own in *la belle France*, maybe a Paris pied-à-terre on the île Saint-Louis or in Montmartre. But in the end they were lured by the azure skies and perfumed air of Provence, and an offer too good to pass up.

Several months earlier, on Simca's patio in southern France, warmed by the sun and not a little wine, Julia and Paul decided this was their paradise, so they meandered through nearby country towns looking for something for sale. Valbonne. Opio. Mougins. Every charming old stone house they looked at turned out to be more picturesque than livable. But Simca's husband, Jean, had a proposal. Why not build a house here at Bramafam, his family's property? They could design it to suit themselves. The land would be leased, and return to his family when they tired of it.

Little chance of that. Julia had fallen for the South of France on her first trip there, in the winter of 1949. Bright blue skies, views of distant mountains, and year-round fields of lavender and roses took her back to childhood summers on the California coast. Paul, with his painter's eye, was equally enthralled. They sealed the deal with a handshake on the spot.

The house would be almost paid for by sales of *Mastering*, already in its sixth printing. And it wasn't hard to rationalize the expense of a second home, since they were already planning a second cookbook. It would be much easier to walk the few yards to the side door of Simca's kitchen than to send reams of recipes back and forth across the Atlantic, as they had for so many years.

They were only too happy to leave the oversight of the crusty local builders to Jean, and on this first inspection trip, everything was just as they had imagined: a room for Paul to paint and putter, a private nook in Julia's bedroom for her books and typewriter, and a compact kitchen, all on one floor. They'd even have room for a guest or two, and more if Paul bunked in a little *cabanon*, a onetime shepherd's hut a few yards from the house.

For months after they returned to Cambridge, Julia kept a letter from Simca tacked to her office wall. It was filled with local gossip, the adventures of her dog, Phano, and relief that the carpenters and plumbers had packed up their tools and were finally gone, along with the dust and noise. Only one more thing would make the dream house complete. Simca closed with the best news of all: "Madame Pussy cat had two kittens with her little mate, so you'll have a pussy-cat for your arrival in December and to chase the mice at La Pitchoune." At last, purrfection.

LE PETIT PRINCE

JULIA'S FACE FLOODED with happiness every time she thought about going "home" to France once again. "La Peetch" would be the respite she and Paul craved from the whirlwind of activity that had begun with a book review program on what Paul described as "an egghead public television station" in Boston. She had cooked an omelette on a hot plate but got so carried away with the demonstration, she forgot to plug her own book. One bowled-over viewer wrote to food critic Craig Claiborne and demanded that he review a book by a big, strange woman she saw on TV. Shortly after, Claiborne's rave review of *Mastering the Art of French Cooking* appeared in the *New York Times*. Soon, The Book was flying off shelves and Julia had a television program of her own.

By 1965, "the French Chef" was finishing her third season, well on her way to becoming a TV star, and while she was eager to share her enthusiasm for the pleasures of the table, the nonstop activity—shopping, scriptwriting, rehearsing, schlepping gear from home, and promotional events—took a toll. The public couldn't get enough, leaving her and Paul with little time for themselves. And no time or place in her hectic life for a house cat, so she was counting the days until they left for their getaway in Provence, where a kitten was waiting.

Since they would be gone for months, Paul was trying to shoehorn an entire household into their battered trunks—aspirin, toothpaste, toilet paper (the soft American kind), and way too many clothes, including heavy New England overcoats, just in case. Plus his painting supplies, the skillets and gadgets she couldn't live without, and pegboard hooks to hang them on, just like the ones in the Cambridge kitchen. Fortunately, he told his brother, one crucial item had been taken care of: "Arrangements for a pussy-cat have been laid on."

When they arrived in Cannes, several of the trunks were missing, especially worrisome since they held Julia's precious recipe notes for the sequel she had nicknamed "Son of *Mastering*." But nothing could dim the excitement as they drove up to their own little piece of Provence for the first time as homeowners. There, just fifty yards from Simca's old stone farmhouse, stood la Peetch with the afternoon sun glinting off the tile roof and freshly painted green shutters. Paul thought the house looked "smiling & scrubbed behind the ears, as glad to see us as we were to see it."

They were greeted by the usual tsunami of barking, tail wagging, and *miaou*ing, and the yelps of an exuberant new puppy. As bonjours and air kisses flew, Julia looked around hopefully for the special poussiequette Simca had promised. Finally, she spotted a pair of bright eyes calmly studying the newcomers from the safety of the stone steps, as if waiting for a formal introduction.

Julia knew the white, black, and brown kitty was The One when he jumped down, rubbed against her ankles, and made a quizzical trilling sound. This people-loving kitten had already acquired a reputation as a Prince Charming who could coax treats from anyone and who ruled the whole menagerie with, as Paul proudly noted, "the loudest purr in Christendom." Julia happily surrendered to his charms and decided to name him "le Petit Prince." He was the first in a line of la Peetch cats over the years to answer to that noble name.

Julia and Paul were bone-tired from the long travel day, but relieved when they got word that their precious trunks had been found at the station. They would collect them in a few days when Julia made the first of her weekly trips to Elizabeth Arden for her *mise en plis*, her curly do.

That evening, Simca invited them for a sumptuous meal marked by several rounds of welcoming toasts. In a pleasant after-dinner buzz, Julia and Paul ended their first la Peetch day on their own terrace, drinking in the sweet night air. The lights of the tiny village of Plascassier shone across the valley and stars glimmered in the cobalt sky. Their new *amour*, le Petit Prince, padded out from the shadows of the mulberry tree, leaped nimbly onto Julia's lap, and purred so loudly Paul feared he might wake the neighbors.

Once again, Julia rested in the embrace of her three loves—an adoring spouse, *la belle France*, and a poussiequette of her own.

Bienvenue!

CHRISTMAS WAS JUST around the corner and the three
"mad women of La Peetch"—Julia, Simca, and Avis DeVoto,
their friend and agent who'd come from Boston for the
holidays—were as excited as *les enfants* waiting for *le Père Noël*.
It was also foie gras season, and the trio of cooks couldn't wait
to get their hands on the quivery pink livers. In a raucous mix
of English and French they argued about which delectable
dishes to cook up for their holiday feast. Would they grind
it with truffles for spreading on croutons? Would they blend
it with prunes to stuff the traditional holiday goose? Would
there be any left when they were done tasting?

To a stranger it sounded chaotic, everyone talking
at once above the sounds of slicing, dicing, pounding,
and sautéing. But to Paul's practiced ear, and from the
safe distance of his den, it was "a jolly, pleasant symphony
accompanied by the smell of hot olive oil and a sense of
gustatory goodies to come."

The feline residents saw no point in waiting. They
wanted their goodies, and they wanted them *meow*! Banished
from the kitchen and wild with the scent of goose liver, the
cats hurled themselves at the door, sticking like magnets to
the screen. Unmoved, the three cooks just raised their voices
a notch to drown out the din. A pampered Petit Prince was
especially incensed at being exiled from his domain, but for
once Julia ignored her favorite's pleas. She was methodically
making notes in her looping script about each step in the
cooking process. She didn't want to miss a chance to learn
something from this boisterous foray into foie gras.

Julia and Simca carried on about the best way to temper

the assertive taste of goose liver: Add cognac, port, or Madeira? Which spices? How much pork fat? Such spirited debate was nothing new. The strong-willed partners kept up a friendly battle over how to cook every dish. Simca insisted that every recipe be authentically French, but Julia cared more that American cooks be able to easily duplicate it with supermarket ingredients. With a best-selling book and a wildly popular cooking show, Julia was now more confident challenging Simca. They argued as if lives were at stake, but in the end they always worked out a compromise, because they kept their eyes on the prize: How does it taste?

The bond between them was wide and deep. They shared a passion for France, for fabulous food and teaching others how to make it—and for cats. They even shared joint custody of a favorite kitty. When the big black-and-white cat stayed with Simca, she answered to the name Whiskey, and at la Peetch, Julia called her Minoir. They were both taken with her dainty habits. She liked to watch TV, strike dramatic poses, and drink water from a glass at the dinner table.

As the dinner hour approached on Christmas Eve, the whole house smelled of goose cracklings, and Paul followed his nose to the kitchen, where the three triumphant cooks stood back admiring their elegant pâtés. Paul popped open a Dom Pérignon to salute their team effort. The not-so-happy cats, still pouting and pacing outside the door, had failed to melt any hearts.

It was a grand Christmas dinner, everyone agreed, including the cats, who, in the spirit of the season, forgave all after they feasted on the remains of the gloriously golden goose. But some cats were more equal than others. Only le Petit Prince tasted the divine pâté.

Whiskey/Minoir

MINOU *MALADE*

JUPAUL TOOK CHARGE of the animal kingdom when
Simca was away teaching in Paris, and it kept them hopping:
"What with cats and dogs and feeding them, we are a veritable
veterinary establishment right here!" With so many needy
critters around, work on the final editing of Julia's *French Chef
Cookbook* slowed to a crawl. The cats were happy, but her New
York publisher not so much. Julia shrugged: "*Voilà—la vie!*"

One day she dashed off a distressed note to Simca.
One of her favorites, the big gray Minou, looked *très malade*.
"Yesterday he was the most miserable eye-streaming old pussy
imaginable—when they say 'sick as a cat' he was it."

She and Paul dropped everything, bundled the poor

thing in an old blanket, and nestled him on the backseat of the Peugeot. He was too sick to put up much of a fight. They shooed his *miaou*ing posse out of the way and took off for the nearest vet, in Grasse, where they were alarmed to hear that a dangerous virus was making the rounds of neighboring farms.

Julia could hardly bear to look into Minou's soulful eyes when they had to leave him overnight, but she was anxious to get home, suddenly fearful for her Little Prince. She watched over him all night as he became listless and wracked by fits of sneezing. In the morning, another frantic ride to Grasse with an unwilling passenger curled in her lap. She stroked his head and urged Paul to please take the twisty country roads just a little faster.

After the Little Prince got a shot of antibiotics, she insisted on taking him home to his castle, where she could administer megadoses of motherly love. For days she and Paul nervously followed the other kitties around the yard listening for any tiny *achoo!* The pussycat plague eventually ran its course, but not before she had to give Simca the sad news that her handsome gray cat did not survive. The medicine came too late, and when he refused even the chicken liver pâté she brought from home, they had to face the awful truth that this Minou had run out of lives. They were devastated: "A very sad business, and we both cried, in fact I am still crying."

Their only solace was a more hopeful prognosis for their own poussiequette, although it was still touch and go. "The darling Petit Prince has had his third injection and will take some medicine for four days. . . . We pray he will be all right, and shall watch him carefully." Their prayers were answered. The vet marveled at the miraculous recovery and gave full credit to Julia's potent brand of TLC.

LE PETIT PRINCE, the kitty with the powerful purr, was the first in a cavalcade of cats Julia pampered at la Pitchoune. Only Paul knew how deep Julia's attachment was to each of them. He confided to his twin, "A cat—any cat—is necessary to Julia's inner satisfaction."

When they returned to Cambridge each year, their sadness at leaving a special cat eased only when Simca wrote that their kitty had been coaxed into rejoining the *miaou*ing chorus at her kitchen door. "Your poussiequette stayed in front of la Pitchoune for 48 hours, always hoping to see the door open, but he didn't want to come, despite our appeals. We had to take him in our arms and carry him into the house so that he'd finally agree to eat. *Alors*, then he did justice to his dinner, and now rests for the night in the kitchen waiting for breakfast."

Letters between the two partners crossed the Atlantic almost daily, packed with recipes and notes that kept their cookery bookery enterprise humming. Julia's jammed typewritten pages and Simca's scrawls in a mélange of French and English captured the daily rhythms of their lives, spiced with local gossip and the doings of their favorite cats. No surprise, the subject was often the capricious feline palate.

Julia: "How is my pussycat (I think of her every time I throw out a boiled chicken neck!)"

Simca: "La Minimouche behaves herself very well, demands her share at dinnertime and waits until she has been fully served. . . . She looks splendid—let's hope she doesn't become enormous."

Handle with care

Julia: "How is our Minimouche? Is she getting very big? I
hope so, as I adore great big poussiequettes."

Simca ruefully replied that Julia's kitty was too much the
gourmand and sometimes resorted to thievery despite her
generous portions. One day, in the blink of an eye, she gobbled
half a pastry tart that was waiting to be garnished. Julia was
amused by the antics of her little thief: "Our Poussiequette
sounds magnifique."

While on vacation at the log cabin Paul and Charlie built

Julia with her sous chef in Maine

in Maine, Julia wrote letters to Simca that filled her in on the status of her extended family of cats: "PS: The two pussies here, Pewter and Copper, are beginning to show their age a bit, both are 14, and though still catching mice, are beginning to look big and ruffled and a bit elderly."

She enjoyed her foster kitties but pined for news of her true loves at la Peetch. She implored Simca for reassurance that out of sight did not mean out of mind. Or heart.

Julia: "We do hope Minimouche will remember us some months from now?? Perhaps we should rush over for 2 days to refresh her memory."

Simca: "Your pussycat hasn't forgotten you because this grand cat is constantly parked between la Pitchoune and le Mas, in expectation of your arrival."

Julia: "How good it will be to see our dear ones. . . . Tell Poussiquette to get herself ready for us."

As the time for the reunion approached, Julia couldn't contain her excitement: "Please tell Minimouche that we are almost on our way."

In her last letter to Simca before departing Boston, Julia looked forward to a kitty welcoming party: "Shall you be bringing your little poussiequette? We hope so. I shall stop at Le Casino in Cannes and get some raw liver *pour enjôler* [to entice] Mlle Minimouche who will have forgotten us. "

No chance of that. At the sound of that familiar high-pitched trill, Julia's poussiequette bounded out of the bushes and raced up the path to her customary post in front of la Pitchoune. While the liver was lovely, there was really no need for gifts. Julia's kitchen door was open again at long last.

WHILE MOST COUNTRY cats never know where their next meal is coming from, the Bramafam kitties had it made, wearing a path between the kitchens of two world-class cooks who were both gaga over felines. One scrawny cat called Minimere was a mother lode of kittens over the years. Julia had a soft spot for the "Little Mama" because she knew that as long as the fertile feline stayed around, she'd never run out of poussiequettes.

Back in Cambridge Julia looked forward to the frequent birth announcements from Simca: "La Minimere has brought 3 kittens since this morning: a light gray one, like herself; a white and gray one; and an all-black one." A happy Julia wrote back at once asking which one would be her special poussiequette: "We need a tough cat (*un dur*) who adores people, who is a gourmand, who is jolly and playful and who likes to walk with us, and wants to be with us every minute." As the matriarch of the Bramafam kitty clan, Simca took her matchmaking seriously and always found the perfect fit.

One summer when Julia and Paul arrived at la Peetch for a short stopover, Minimere was predictably pregnant. Since the cat was eating for two or three or more, Julia filled her bowl to overflowing and rubbed her back until she was drowsy. Soon there would be new kittens to love. But because they were leaving soon to vacation with friends in Norway, they worried that the Little Mama might choose their house for her lying-in hospital.

JuPaul were no match for the wily mother-to-be. On the prowl for a secluded spot to deliver her brood, Minimere lurked near the kitchen door for a chance to sneak inside and settle in a half-open bureau drawer, a cupboard left ajar, or a soft basket of laundry. When Simca knocked, carrying a warm *tarte aux poires*, the cat slipped in and disappeared down the hall.

The next evening, amid a soothing soundtrack of twilight warblers, Julia sat correcting recipes while Paul jotted notes to Charlie. Suddenly an avalanche of tumbling bottles, splintering glass, and an ear-piercing "Yowwwwl!" jolted them to their feet. As they raced toward the din, a wild-eyed Minimere darted by as fast as her drooping tummy would allow.

The clever kitty had found an open closet, clawed her way up the coats, and built a cozy nest for her confinement on top of some bottles Paul had stashed on the shelf. Paul and Julia groaned at the mess but had to admire Minimere's persistence and agility, and though it took the rest of the evening to clean up the sticky shards of Cinzano bottles, they counted their blessings. At least it wasn't one of Julia's precious Château d'Yquems. Never ones to cry over spilled wine or pass up a chance to celebrate, they opened the last unbroken bottle and toasted the mother-to-be.

When the spooked cat failed to appear for breakfast the next morning, Paul assumed she was "spawning future bottle-breakers in the hollow of some olive tree." They knew the proud mama would soon come around toting her kittens by the scruff of the neck. When she dropped the *miaou*ing balls of fluff at the kitchen door, Julia would be ready with some choice chicken parts and saucers of cream. Like any doting grandma, she couldn't wait.

Mama-to-be up a tree

Eyes on the prize

"LIKE PUSSIES IN CATNIP"

THE MINUTE ANOTHER season of *The French Chef* was in the
can, Julia and Paul started packing for Provence, where the
pace of life slowed. Once settled in their snug retreat, Julia
jotted to Freddie, "Left Paris absolutely bone-chill-frigid at
3 PM, came down out of clear blue sky w/ sun! Glad to be home
w/ our own Pussy, our China tea, our houselet, our quiet, our
sun, our flowers. . . ." And she added a bright red marginal note:
"Our new pussy is a dear—tiger back and white feet & face &
little tiger mustache."

They named her Minimouche, and like all kittens, she
was in perpetual motion. As soon as Paul opened the shutters
in the morning, she shot outside like an arrow toward a

bull's-eye—a ring of yellow pansies around the olive tree—while Julia sang out, "*Alors, Minimouche, fais oui-oui!*" The kitten helpfully "watered" the flowers, then raced back for breakfast. On warm days they ate in the shade of the mulberry tree and lingered over the *Nice-Matin* newspaper, while the kitty chased lizards in the sun.

When Paul retired to his studio, Julia went to her alcove to tap out recipes. On a quest for the holy grail of baking, the secret to making real French bread in American ovens, she churned out golden crusty loaves almost every day. Even as he fought an expanding waistline, Paul was only too happy to assess the merits of each buttery loaf: "I shall eat it, my pleasure all the greater because of the partner facing me across the table."

At lunchtime, he headed toward the *slap-slap* of Julia pummeling her yeasty dough. The insistent *miaou*s of a hungry cat nipping at her ankles set off a round of futile but fond chiding: "*Mimi! Ferme ta petite bouche! C'est défendu de faire ce bruit. Non, non, non!*" (Mimi, shut your little mouth. I forbid you to make such noise. No, no, no!) Her falsetto scoldings made more racket than the cat's begging, but she and Minimouche both seemed fond of their little game.

After a half tumbler of Côtes de Provence and a hunk of bread slathered with sweet butter, it was back to the studio, where Paul often painted until his fingertips grew numb. Meanwhile, Julia and Minimouche grabbed *un petit somme* (a little catnap) while waiting for the next batch of dough to rise.

In the late afternoon they took long walks with the kitty prancing along beside them. They loved to watch their high-leaping pussy pirouette after butterflies and surge up and down in the high grass with a rolling rhythm that reminded them of an antelope in the savanna. Paul, ever the worrier, fretted that their kitten might stray too far, but she always found her way back to them and flopped at their feet panting like a dog. The blissful days followed "like pearls on a priceless necklace," he wrote. "We fairly roll in them, like pussies in catnip."

Some winter evenings the fierce mistral winds set the trees dancing and rattled the shutters, making their *petite maison* seem more like Wuthering Heights. They lit the fireplace and tried to ignore the howling and creaking. While Julia mashed garlic for ragout Provençale, Paul read to her from a back issue of the *New Yorker*. If they could get a signal, they watched the news flickering on a small black-and-white TV.

Minimouche had little patience for fashionably late dinners and by eight was loudly complaining, which drew another affectionate scold: "*Qu'est que c'est que cette bruit, petit monstre?*" (What's up with this noise, little monster?) But some juicy giblets always landed in her dish.

When the winds calmed and heavens cleared, they donned heavy sweaters to sip a nightcap on the patio under a moonless sky. In winter the Big Dipper hung low over la Peetch, stars flashed like a million fireflies, and an occasional satellite slowly arced toward the horizon while the tiny purring machine settled in Julia's lap.

After they turned in for the night, the kitty sometimes disappeared into the blackness and they speculated about her mysterious nocturnal life. Did she hitch a ride on a broomstick with one of the local witches? The village gossips whispered about a certain farmer's wife who was said to practice the black arts. Or was Minimouche headed for a secret tryst, a rendezvous with a *petit ami*? Time would tell.

"NO CATERWAULING"

THE STRING OF wonder days ended when Julia and Paul returned to Boston to finish *A Dinner at the White House*, a TV special that aired in March of 1968 and certified her status as a bona fide national treasure. They counted on a quick return to their charmed life in Provence and their Minimouche who, Simca confirmed, was "in a family way."

Julia longed to play midwife, but a routine visit to her doctor brought shocking news. She had breast cancer and would need a radical mastectomy. Although she downplayed its seriousness, Paul, who fretted if his "wifelet" caught a cold or complained of a tummyache, was distraught. But Julia preferred to focus on returning to la Peetch and her poussiequette: "We were so looking forward to being there tomorrow afternoon, standing on that lovely terrace, smelling the lovely air, patting Pastis, stroking Mlle Minimouche."

Typically stoic, Julia determined to put the surgery behind her: "No radiation, no chemotherapy, no caterwauling." As soon as the doctor gave the okay, they flew to Provence for her long recuperation. Monitoring the pussycat pregnancy was just the distraction they needed. She wrote to Simca, who was teaching in Paris, "*Mlle Minimouche de la Brague et de Bramafam-Pitchoune* still has her kittens inside her. Jeanne said we shall have to wait for the turn of the moon! We have set out a nice box for her in *la Poulailler*."

In a corner of the henhouse, they lined a cardboard box with shredded paper and cut a hole just big enough for Minimouche to fit through. When they thought the time was right—eyeing the cat's tummy and not the moon—they nestled the mama-to-be inside the box. But the pampered kitty wasn't accustomed to such rustic accommodations. Paul ruefully wrote Charlie that the kitty was back on their kitchen floor in half an hour.

Everyone in the compound went on kitten watch, but Jeanne, the Bramafam caretaker and font of country wisdom, preached patience and correctly predicted: "Now that the new moon has come the cat will have her kittens." Like proud parents, Paul and Julia announced to family back home the arrival of five adorable kittens on the fourth of May.

The *chatons* were soon all spoken for and Minimouche seemed ready to resume her life—and midnight trysts. Paul thought it was time for permanent birth control, since one

A place in the soleil

Minimere was enough to keep Bramafam in kittens. So off they went, "to Grasse at 8 AM with Julie, carrying our Mini-Mouche imprisoned in a cardboard carton. On its open top was tied a dish-drying rack so she couldn't jump out."

In the coming weeks Julia empathized with her fellow surgery patient. She still wore a rubber sleeve to prevent complications from her own operation, and dutifully performed painful exercises in order to regain full use of her shoulder and arm. Partly to placate a worried Paul, she took long daily naps and let Jeanne help her in the kitchen.

As always, the relaxed rhythms of life at la Peetch cast a restful spell. Summer's full bounty was all around them in alfalfa fields, olive groves, and hillsides covered in every shade of pink. Farm women in big straw hats with white cloth bags around their necks harvested the roses that ended up in the perfume factories in Grasse. Day and night the air smelled of honey.

Gradually Julia found her way back to the kitchen, filling the house with her favorite fragrances: garlic, tomatoes, roasting chickens, and baking apples. The effect was magical for both patients. Paul gleefully reported that one morning, "as though Merlin had waved his wand over her, the little cat walked out of her sick-bay, ate a whole dishful of hamburger, drank half a puddleful of hose-water, rushed up an olive tree & was cured."

In a parallel burst of energy, a reinvigorated Julia began to complain to Paul that she'd had enough of peace and quiet: "Breakfast at the same house, then work, then lunch, then work, then dinner, then work, then bed. Every day the same! No friends, no trips, no nothing!" Paul had to agree that it was time for the "French Cheffie" to return to Cambridge and get back into the thick of things.

"UNE MAISON SANS CHAT . . ."

WHEN JULIA AND Paul returned to Cambridge in the summer of 1968, they landed in the thick of things they hadn't at all expected. Their house on Irving Street was within shouting distance of noisy political protests in Harvard Yard. They sympathized with the antiwar and civil rights demonstrations, but hated the climate of fear. When a brick flew through the window of a Harvard faculty neighbor, Paul decided to install an elaborate burglar alarm.

Feeling vaguely as if their home were under siege, Julia longed for the safety of la Peetch and the comforting companionship of her poussiequette: "We keep thinking we

hear Mlle Minimouche calling to be let in—would that we did."
She missed having a pussycat underfoot at Irving Street, so
when friends asked her to kitty-sit, she jumped at the chance.

Geoffrey arrived one evening in a large blue carrying
case. After formal introductions, both Paul and Julia took an
immediate shine to the big, orange, "somewhat neurotic" cat.
Geoffrey needed pills twice a day, and given their advanced
kitty nursing skills, they felt sure pill-pushing would be a
snap. On the first try, Geoffrey opened wide, said "Meow!"
and with perfect timing, Paul stuffed in a large capsule. *Pas
de problème!* He smugly repeated the technique the next day,
and the day after that. Later in the week, Julia's slippered feet
felt something squish. Looking behind the sofa, she found
Geoffrey's entire stash of soggy pills and came up with a more
foolproof delivery system. She wrapped the pill in goose liver
pâté and tossed it in the air. Geoffrey snapped it up before it
hit the ground. *Fait accompli.*

Julia was used to hearing her voice compared to a foghorn,
flute, sliding trombone, or worse, so she got a kick out of the
odd sounds that came from Geoffrey's voice box. She chortled
to Simca that when he wanted to roam the neighborhood, "he
comes up to say 'Qweek, I want to go out.' Then he disappears
under the bushes and we find him later sitting by the front
door, saying 'Qweek, I want to come in.' "

In no time at all, the visiting royalty ruled the Child
household. He thrived on his vastly improved menus and grew
more fond of his foster parents by the day. When Julia and
Paul went out for an evening, Geoffrey faithfully waited for
them on the pillar beside their front gate like a majestic stone
lion. When Charlie and Freddie came for an overnight stay
with their overly affectionate Briard, Geoffrey tolerated the

slobbery canine but seemed glad to see them go so he could reclaim his privileged status.

A short time after bidding Geoffrey a sad adieu, Julia welcomed another houseguest: "A little white pussy cat has come to make her home with us for a few days; she had been abandoned, and was so loving and appealing we could not resist." She bathed the bedraggled orphan, fattened her up with freshly ground hamburger, and lavished affection on her temporary lap cat until she found it a good home. Word of her hospitality soon hit the feline street, bringing a string of strays to her door. One liked to take his afternoon naps in a big olive-wood salad bowl on Julia's pantry shelf.

She embraced them all: "I do like a house with a pussy in it!" Every furry visitor proved her mantra, *"Une maison sans chat, c'est la vie sans soleil."* (A house without a cat is life without sunshine.)

Let me in, s'il vous plaît

AFTER A FEW years of black-and-white reruns, *The French Chef* made a triumphant return in luscious color. Viewers thrilled to the eye-popping red berries and snowy *crème pâtissière* of Julia's *tarte aux fraises*, the electric green of blanched haricots, and the rainbow hues of fresh mountain trout. A much larger budget let Julia and Paul take a production crew to France so viewers could see for themselves all the places she'd been breathlessly describing.

Off they went in the spring of 1970 to the dining room in Rouen where she had first tasted heavenly French food. They filmed Chef Dorin creating his famous pressed duck tableside, and then it was on to Paris to watch baker Raymond Calvel pull trays of baguettes from his brick oven. Julia led viewers through the aisles of Dehillerin, the "Old Curiosity Shop" of cookware, stuffed floor to ceiling with every gadget under the sun.

In Provence they explored the sprawling market on the edge of the Old City in Nice, a noisy bazaar of stalls heaped with the bounty of the countryside. Julia always stopped there on the way to la Peetch to buy armloads of tulips and tins of liver pâté to placate her kitty after a long absence. Close to home, they visited the ancient stone olive press at Opio to scoop giant ripe olives from a barrel of brine with a special olive-wood ladle.

Everywhere Julia went, she ran into "J-Ws," a friendly but persistent gaggle of Julia-Watchers who greeted her like an old friend. Even in busy airports, parents thrust children upon her for a snapshot and regaled her with their own culinary adventures: "Finally I can make crepes!" And misadventures:

"My soufflés just won't pouf up like yours!" Maître d's and waiters were excited to see her, and other diners always had to know what *she* was eating. Once in an airport restaurant, an Irish priest stopped by her table to express the gratitude so many seemed to feel: "God bless you, Miss Childs, 'tis a noble thing yer doin'."

Julia was always gracious, though she and Paul sometimes ducked their heads when they heard loud American voices approaching. During the filming in Nice, a woman interrupted a crew lunch to exclaim, "My goodness! It's Julier Chiles! . . . My daughter and I watch your program every Thursday night back home in Michigan. My friends just won't *believe* it when I tell them I actually *saw* you in person!"

At times fan affection went too far. After the TV tour of Provence aired, the more intrepid J-Ws showed up in the untouristy village of Plascassier. Ignoring the gate, they trudged up the private road to snoop around the Bramafam compound, peering through the windows and French doors. The cognoscenti could tell which house was hers by the cats lounging on the patio or purring by the kitchen door. If Julia was home, she'd stop what she was doing to bellow a hearty *Bonjooour!* She'd sign the books they lugged and pose for "just one" picture, before politely excusing herself and sending the starstruck intruders on their way.

When fellow cat lovers discovered she was one of them, they showered her with cat trinkets, hotpads, aprons, nightshirts, and all kinds of cat-themed clothing, along with pictures of themselves with their own cats. One fan, who somehow learned that one of Julia's Provence cats had died, offered to deliver a silver-haired pussycat "who looks like our dear departed" to the house on Irving Street.

You wash, I'll dry

Sometimes the mail brought strange requests. One writer hoped Julia would endorse her paper on "Cat Cookery," filled with detailed recipes from cultures that viewed cats as suitable dining fare. Julia was repulsed by the whole idea, but still sent the woman a polite "I'll get back to you."

When Julia and her pussycat were shown cooking together in her own kitchen, it struck a chord. One cat-loving cook wrote, "Since I saw you in *Bon Appétit* photographed at your farmhouse in Provence with the cat in the kitchen sink, I have really felt you are my kind of people."

Many fans found a special way to pay homage. For decades, countless well-fed cats from Boston to Bozeman answered to "Julia" when dinner was served.

BY THE SUMMER of 1977, Julia had taped more than two hundred *French Chef* episodes and finished an exhausting tour to promote *From Julia Child's Kitchen*. She and Paul looked forward to the lazy routines at la Peetch—writing letters, pruning rosebushes, and eating lunch under their mulberry tree with a pussycat frolicking nearby.

Paul needed an extended sabbatical even more than Julia. Three years earlier, she'd convinced him to see about the chest pains he kept shrugging off, and he underwent triple bypass surgery. It probably saved his life, but their elation quickly faded. Julia confided to Simca that he had suffered small strokes during the operation and now often complained of being in a mental fog. She feared that her dynamic life partner would never be quite the same.

Mutual adoration society

More damaging than the *crise cardiaque* was the blow to Paul's self-esteem. The eloquent writer who composed poetry in French and English was sometimes at a loss for words, especially when he tried to converse in French, leaving Julia to deal with shopkeepers and train conductors. He often felt frustrated and forlorn in crowds and was happiest filling his days with painting and photography, talents that didn't forsake him. He put his faith in the invigorating air of Provence, which had helped restore Julia to full health after her own surgery.

Their peaceful days were enlivened by the adorable poussiequette Simca had waiting for them. He was a fine striped tiger, Julia bragged in a letter to her cat-loving friend M. F. K. Fisher. In homage to other favorites, they named him Minouche, a cross between "Minou" and "Minimouche," but like all of Julia's kitties, he was usually called by the affectionate Julia-ism "Poussiequette."

Minouche was one of those cats who saw no compelling reason to make up his mind. This feline Hamlet wanted to be in and wanted to be out, as he pleased, and if the nimble puss found a window closed or a door latched, he made his displeasure emphatically clear. He was most vocal in the middle of an afternoon siesta or early-morning snooze. Julia had a habit from their Paris days of padding into Paul's room, setting the alarm for eight, and curling up beside him for a few more z's. The restless Minouche developed his own habit of pouncing at the precise moment they drifted off.

Sleepless, cranky, and exasperated by Minouche's roaming ways, Paul engineered an ingenious solution. It took some patient explaining to the skeptical carpenter who came to install a special window over the kitchen sink that let Minouche come and go as he fancied. It was a win-win.

Minouche could wander in and out to his heart's content, while Julia and Paul could dally in dreamland a bit longer without visits from a perambulating pussycat.

CATS 'N' ROSES

JULIA WAS NOW a genuine superstar, the biggest public television had ever produced. A namesake Muppet lived on Sesame Street, and the real-life Julia cooked spaghetti with Mr. Rogers in his Neighborhood. Later he sent an exuberant mash note that captured her unique appeal for all ages: "Thank you for spaghetti and YOU! . . . You evoke a kind of loving admiration from those you meet. . . . You're a grand person."

The food world, tiny as it was then, recognized a good thing and welcomed her warmly. Until Julia came along, cooking on TV belonged to stern nutritionists or glamour girls like Betty Furness and Bess Myerson, whose culinary expertise began and ended with opening refrigerator doors. The exception was James Beard, who first appeared in the forties on tiny black-and-white screens that could barely contain his ample frame. He invited Julia to teach at his New York cooking school, and became one of her most ardent boosters and a dear friend who happily shared the kitchen limelight. The public found them both endearing—jovial, bighearted, and unpretentious. Julia and Jim made food fun.

JuPaul loved playing host to Jim and other foodies, friends, and family at la Peetch. They took everyone around to their favorite restaurants for a taste of authentic Provençal fare and to lively local festivals. Every spring the Fête de Roses in Grasse celebrated the rose harvest, the sweet-smelling mainstay of the local economy, where visitors sniffed and

swooned over three thousand varieties of blooms. One year the organizers decided to combine the flower show with another wildly popular event, the annual cat show. Well. Julia and Paul thought that was a brilliant idea. Since their first pilgrimage to the Cat Club de Paris expo, they rarely passed one up.

At the "Cat and Roses Show," they hurried past the flowers to get to the real attraction: "The roses were superb, but we were so drawn to those mysterious and fascinating creatures, the cats, that we did only a token walk-past of the roses."

They strolled up and down the aisles, stopping at each

cage so Julia could fuss over the competing kitties. In this temple of cat worship, Julia was like every other acolyte, blending into the crowd, until an American couple recognized the tall woman with the famous falsetto. It was hard to tell who was more agog—the Williamses when they spotted her, or Julia when they introduced her to their magnificent Persian puss. The couple had come a long way to enter him in the show, but now it didn't matter if they won a blue ribbon or not. Running into *the* Julia Child was the prize they'd never forget.

Responding to Julia's breathy oohs and aahs, the bedazzled owners pulled the fluffy cat with the outsize name "Lewishof's Michael" out of his cage so Julia could stroke and hug him. Paul immediately sensed this was a mistake: "I thought for a few minutes I was going to have to use my bull-whip to force her to give it back to Williams, but by an act of immeasurable will-power and renunciation, she returned it."

A few days later they were delighted to read in the local paper that Julia's main squeeze took one of two top prizes at the show. Julia ripped the picture from the paper and tucked it into a letter home, so their Minouche would never find out about her cat-show dalliance with the dashing Persian.

STILL LIFE WITH CAT

AFTER A FIVE-YEAR absence from TV, in 1977 Julia agreed to a new series, *Julia Child & Company*. She'd put on some pounds and vowed to lose them before the camera added even more. Paul was watching the scale too, and lamented that he had to cut back on wine and settle for Château de Pompe, as the French call plain tap water, even when they dined at their friend Roger Vergé's three-star restaurant. As for Minouche,

JuPaul's attempted loss was his gain, and he grew plump on the leftovers and nibbles the three would normally share.

Paul's letters home focused on bigger losses—not just the pounds, but his physical limitations and changes to their peaceful corner of Provence. Paradise was being spoiled by Hollywood-style mansions. The influx of people meant more roads and the blight of transmission lines crisscrossing the hills. On a trip to Nice they were almost run down by American-style rolling carts in a huge new supermarket.

Julia was always more open to the new, especially when it came to gadgets that took the drudgery out of cooking, like the food processor. In a few spins, it could turn out *quenelles de brochet*, those scrumptious poufs that once had her pounding fish until she thought her arms would drop off. But she grumped along with Paul that the French seemed to be turning into convenience cooks. The supermarket was just the latest sign of a creeping Americanization of food.

One of the new things Paul did embrace was a Polaroid camera, despite his purist's disdain for the "point the box and push the button" school of photography. Julia enjoyed the instant gratification of the new camera and got a kick out of taking snapshots of friends, furry and otherwise, who grinned as she sang out, "Smile, and say 'Soufflé'!"

Julia loved to go along on Paul's photo expeditions through the steep limestone hills and sleepy villages. He bragged that she was getting better at picture-taking herself, and it was probably Julia's idea to rope Minouche into an experiment. Why not try to capture the cat as he leaped through his special kitty window? But she grossly underestimated the degree of difficulty. First, catch a wary cat. Second, try to hold on to the squirming, scratching,

*miaou*ing thing while Paul gets into position and checks his light meter. Third, persuade him to vault through the window on cue. Fourth, spend a half hour calling "Here MinoucheMinoucheMinouche" every time he manages to wriggle free and take off after a lizard or bunny or anything else that moves.

When Julia's arms looked like pincushions, Paul took a turn clutching the writhing cat while she snapped the picture, but he had even less luck keeping their hyperactive star calm.

After countless futile shutter clicks, they gave up on the action shot and decided on a simpler pose, Minouche's head framed in the cat window. Julia doled out bits of raw liver and murmured in his ear to keep him from escaping before Paul was ready. They eventually got the shot, but Minouche got all the liver Julia had planned to grind into a luncheon pâté.

When Minouche waddled off for a post–photo session nap, Paul suggested Julia's next subject should be a still life. In a letter to Charlie explaining his picture-taking philosophy, Paul referred to the cat-window episode with droll understatement: "A struggling cat is anything but simple to photograph."

A DANGEROUS RIVAL

ONE MORNING A big black cat with a nasty disposition shattered the peace and quiet of la Peetch. This "monster Beeko" belonged to one of Simca's cooking school students, who stayed in the house down the hill. Soon a feline turf war was on. Beeko crept up to the patio where Minouche lay napping and let fly a barrage of howls and screeches. Since Paul was at his outdoor easel and Julia in the kitchen nearby, Minouche stood his ground—from under a lawn chair, to be sure.

Minouche's calm gaze infuriated Beeko even more. Paul imagined the aggressor's rant: "I'm going to take over! Also all the food around here, and the next time 'I'll beat the beejeesus outa youze!'"

Beeko finally got his chance—Minouche, dozing in the sun all by himself. When the bully lunged at their kitten, Julia rushed out shrieking and waving her whisk. Paul too came running, a dripping paintbrush in one hand and palette knife in the other. Beeko tumbled backward into the thorny rosebushes and whimpered all the way home.

But it wasn't over. Next time, the brute wised up and sneaked in under the radar before Minouche could summon the swat team. The little tiger showed spunk but got the worst of it, a nasty bite on his paw, and had to be quickly bundled off to the vet, who by now knew almost the entire la Peetch kitty corps.

The feisty Minouche had to endure house arrest while his wound healed. He paced and *miaou*ed, and the minute his bandage came off, he leaped out his window into a driving rainstorm, oblivious to the whereabouts of his rival. *Bonne chance!* A lucky break for Minouche. Beeko and his owner had bid adieu to Bramafam.

Soon Julia and Paul were packing up too, heartbroken at leaving their new favorite behind. "Our poussiequette is adorable, and we simply hate to give him up—but shall return him regretfully to Bramafam Saturday evening. How can we

Our french pussy: It's name is Minouche. Please send him to us in Cambridge after we get back. (The photo, not the cat, though we wish we could put a stamp on him & send him too.)

Polaroid

R

thank you enough—*comment vous dire à quel point*—we have appreciated this priceless loan! Merci, merci!"

Paul worried for Minouche. What would he do without Julia, "who feeds him and talks to him and pats him, and strokes him, and kisses his head's top-knot . . . if the closed kitchen window (the pussy's exit and entrance-system) is unfriendly, and firmly shut, poor puss!" He scribbled a unique solution next to a photo of their kitty and sent it to Charlie— they could put a stamp on him and send him by airmail to Cambridge.

But mailing Minouche was wishful thinking. He'd have to settle for Simca's warm kitchen, kisses, and cuisine until he heard JuPaulski's Peugeot rumble up the dusty road to la Peetch once again.

"BOUTEZ EN AVANT!"

JULIA'S RESPITES AT la Peetch energized her, and after several weeks of R and R, she was ready for action, merrily plunging into the next TV or writing project. For Paul, it was getting harder to pick up and move across the ocean as often as they once did. With age he became less tolerant of the Provençal heat, but New England winters were hardly more attractive. Even though France would always exert a strong pull, the sunny shores of California beckoned. So in 1981 they bought a condo on the coast near Santa Barbara where they could spend the winter months and one day retire.

For Julia, it was a kind of homecoming. Their new place was near the spot where the McWilliams family had rented a summerhouse and Julia spent carefree days on the beach. The sea breezes and rolling hills covered with olive groves, lavender, and roses felt like paradise—Provence without the hassles of overseas travel and separation from family. Paul made his last trip to la Peetch in 1986 and, with his health failing, entered a nursing home a few years later. Julia returned to their hillside hideaway several more times, but it wasn't the same without her Paulski, and she always hurried home to be near him.

Paul once wrote, "Due to Julia's temperament she believes that everything will always be OK everywhere, at all times." Far from a Pollyanna, she was deeply pained by Paul's long, slow decline but kept her sorrow to herself. She made sure he was included in her cooking demonstrations and guest appearances for as long as possible, and when he could no longer keep up, she visited, often twice a day, and faithfully phoned when she was traveling. Paul died in May 1994, and she blew a kiss as she scattered his ashes into the Atlantic near their Maine cabin.

She composed her best tribute to Paul in the 1968 *French Chef Cookbook*: "Paul Child, the man who is always there: porter, dishwasher, official photographer, mushroom dicer and onion chopper, editor, fish illustrator, manager, taster, idea man, resident poet, and husband."

Though she grieved the loss of her soul mate, Julia was never one to look back. Her gaze was firmly set on the horizon, and in time she embraced a busy bicoastal life. There were more cooking shows with new partners like Jacques Pépin, books to write and promote, and galas for pet projects like the American Institute of Wine and Food, an organization born at her dinner table. She was constantly looking for new ways to spread the gospel of good food, the life mission she discovered with Paul and Minette in Paris all those years ago. In her last decades, Julia lived her favorite motto: *"Boutez en avant!"* (Charge ahead!)

5.

FROM CAMBRIDGE TO CALIFORNIA: A HOMECOMING

Julia and her kitchen Graces

A TRIO OF cats in a field of bright green asparagus peered out from a painting in Julia's Cambridge kitchen. One friend thought they represented the Greek goddesses of Joy, Beauty, and Good Cheer, the three Graces whose dancing charms enlivened temple feasts. While Julia's "Graces" couldn't link paws and cavort around her kitchen, their bright-eyed gaze never failed to make her smile as she cooked a lovely meal for friends and served it with a jaunty *"Bon appétit!"*

The artist was Rosemary Manell, one of Julia's dearest friends, who was equally nutty about cats. They met when their Foreign Service husbands took them to France, where they bonded over French cooking and champagne. Both were tall California girls who shared a taste for adventure and an earthy sense of humor. While Julia's career in food blossomed, Rosie lived an artist's life in California. But when Julia needed an all-around kitchen helper, Rosie was at her side, her indispensable right hand, bringing artistic flair to food design for her TV shows and books. The *Cats with Asparagus* painting may have been inspired by Blooper, Rosie's gray *chat de gouttière*, who loved to eat asparagus, but only, she claimed, if it was perfectly cooked. A French foodie cat to the core.

Since a live-in cat was still out of the question for the globe-trotting Julia, she filled the house with faux felines. Kitty magnets clung to the refrigerator door, a neon-orange cat stared from a shopping bag, and pot holders in various feline poses collected near the stove. The Kliban cartoon cat crooning "Love to eat them mousies. . . ." shared wall space with a pensive photo by Paul of a silhouetted Minou. A sinuous glass cat reclined on a shelf, and Julia's muse, the wooden marmalade cat she carted around to TV kitchens, leaned against the window, ready for duty.

It didn't have far to travel. The rambling Colonial often doubled as a studio for photo shoots and TV shows, like the series *In Julia's Kitchen with Master Chefs*. Now in her eighties, Julia liked to work at home. When she called, some of the biggest names in the culinary world showed up at her door, thrilled to be invited into the inner sanctum. Energized by cooking with new friends, Julia wasn't ready to limit her role to host-observer, an "Alistair Cookie." To the delight of her fans, she more than kept pace with chefs half her age.

If they expected to be wowed by acres of granite and high-end cooking gear, they were in for a surprise. Her kitchen was like Julia herself, unpretentious and welcoming. Shooting in the smallish room proved a challenge, but it was handy for Julia, who could go up to her room—not to nap, but to type book notes between takes.

Not far from the kitchen, the living room floor was a tangle of black cables tethered to hefty video cameras. Monitors and audio decks teetered on tables as a dozen staffers murmured into headsets, while Julia coordinated her assistants—literally sous chefs, down below in the basement prep kitchen. Her trusty aides performed with the precision of a drill team under the direction of their cheery drum major: "That looks just yummy, dearies!" From dawn till dusk, the kitchen elves prepared the recipes in stages, then sent them up to the kitchen "studio," where Julia and her master chef du jour finished the lesson for the cameras.

Famous chefs weren't the only ones vying to be invited into Julia's kitchen—neighborhood cats were always trying to get into the act. On an unusually hectic production day, one

Ready for my close-up, Mrs. Child

of the furry Irving Street habitués, drawn by delectable smells but denied his customary access, paced furiously outside the kitchen window. The guest chef, Leah Chase, the "Queen of Creole Cooking," was preparing Southern fried chicken that called for very hot oil and split-second timing. The director fretted about overtime and the cost of multiple takes, so each step had to be precisely choreographed, building to the climactic moment when chicken leg hits smoking oil.

The director finally barked, "Quiet on the set. Cameras rolling." Then, with a broad smile into the camera's red light, America's beloved kitchen guru began her umpteenth show. "Hel-*lo*, I'm *Joo*-lya Child!" Everything was going according to plan, until she picked up a flour-dredged drumstick and dropped it into the bubbling oil. At that moment, the hungry cat pawing at the window let out such an ear-splitting yowl even the basement crew froze. Had there been a terrible accident? Boiling oil spilled? Fingers burned? Julia realized the wailing came from the outraged pussycat on the sill. Everything came to a halt until she got her gasping whoops under control, fished the soggy drumstick from the pot, and reheated the oil.

Take two: coat the chicken leg, shake off excess flour, and drop it into the smoking fat. On cue, the frantic cat did another take of his own, scratching at the windowpane and growling when the chicken hit the oil. "Cut!" Do it again. And again, until they were almost out of drumsticks.

Finally Julia saw that her team didn't think the cat's antics were as hilarious as she did. They were stymied—no one wanted to confront the testy, hungry feline. Julia came up with a surefire plan for relocating the demanding heckler. Send someone down the alley toting a steaming bucket of outtakes—extra-crispy, paw-lickin' good, Southern fried, master chef carryout.

AN ALARMING POUSSIEQUETTE

WHEN THE TV crews cleared out, life on Irving Street resumed a quieter pace. Friends were still in and out, and Julia's nephew David stayed in the guest room during graduate school, keeping her company, especially at dinnertime. But with no Paul around to share a laugh and lift a postproduction flute of champagne, Julia's housekeeper thought the place needed more than cat tchotchkes to liven things up. One day she arrived for work with a surprise tucked in her cleaning supplies.

The scene was eerily similar to that fateful day forty years earlier when Julia's Parisian *femme de ménage* presented her with something she didn't know she needed until she laid eyes on Minette. Julia plucked a buff-colored Persian kitten out of the bucket and beamed. Before she picked a name, she recalled Paul's astute anatomy lesson. This poussiequette was definitely a Minou, not a Minette.

The rambunctious kitten loved to tear up and down the stairs and defy gravity, soaring from the newel post to the top of the bookcase. It wasn't long before the little acrobat ran afoul of the burglar alarm. Julia tried her best to train Minou to pussyfoot around the sensors that would trigger an alert, but it was useless to reason with this highflier in the throes of a kitty-fit.

When the phone rang in the middle of the night, a groggy Julia had to reassure worried security guards she was in no danger. It was just an irrepressible kitten making his nocturnal rounds. After multiple midnight alarms, Julia reluctantly called her sister in California. Would Dort be a dear and adopt the lively kitten? He's so much like that Roo de Loo rascal, Minette. The sisters reminisced about those long-ago French lessons punctuated by kitty love bites and telltale potatoes that turned up amid the lingerie. Dort, the lifelong animal lover, immediately said "*Oui!*" Minou felt right at home with someone who looked and sounded so much like Julia, but Julia sorely missed the fluffy troublemaker. When the sisters held their frequent gabfests, Julia always asked Dort to put her on speakerphone so Minou wouldn't forget her.

In 2002, Julia moved to Santa Barbara for good and donated the Irving Street house to her alma mater, Smith College. A cadre of museum curators descended on the famous kitchen and meticulously documented everything in it, from the secondhand Garland range she bought for their first house in Georgetown for $429—a huge sum in 1956—to the marble mortar Paul lugged from the Paris flea market and the blue KitchenAid mixer hand-painted by Rosie Manell, plus every gizmo "Jackdaw Julie" had gathered over the years. They bubble-wrapped the cats that romped across her black refrigerator, the *Cats with Asparagus* painting, and the TV kitty mascot, and loaded the treasures into a moving van headed to the Smithsonian Institution in Washington, D.C., where it was all lovingly reassembled.

Before the exhibit opened to the public, Julia toured it with family and a few close friends. She was tickled by the detailed re-creation—everything exactly where it belonged, down to the last tea towel. In the flood of happy memories, her thoughts turned to her *cheri*. Leaning on a friend's arm, she confided, "Oh, if only Paul could be here to see this. He would be so thrilled."

As are the thousands of fans who make the pilgrimage to Julia's kitchen each year. Gazing at the big wooden table and well-worn cookware, visitors yearn for the only thing that's missing—Julia herself, filling the room with joyous exuberance. As they exit, visitors sometimes leave offerings—a champagne flute or stick of butter—or simply blow a kiss and whisper, "*Bon appétit!*"

TRAVELS WITH JULIA

EVEN IN HER late eighties, Julia's idea of a perfect afternoon was speeding along in a red pickup truck on a winding country road she'd never been down before. Or waiting to board a plane, boat, or train that would take her to whatever was next. Amid the vineyards and sprawling country estates near Santa Barbara, NO TRESPASSING signs were meant for people with no imagination and PRIVATE PROPERTY postings surely only a suggestion. She egged on timid drivers to ignore keep-out signs and drive just a little faster. After all, she brightly reasoned, who wouldn't be happy to see Julia Child coming up the drive?

She said she'd already clocked as many miles as an astronaut, but traveled much more lightly. Her suitcase held a skirt, a few pairs of slacks, some brightly patterned blouses, black Mary Janes with "straps to hold your feet in," sneakers, a girdle, and makeup. The moment she snapped the case shut, she could and did go everywhere. Moving through an airport, she invariably attracted a flotilla of fans that swelled as it passed each gate. Everyone thought of her as a friend or favorite auntie and wanted to chat. Oblivious to the clock, she'd graciously pose for pictures. If she discovered a fellow cat lover, she would pull out her day planner and, like any proud grandmother, show off snapshots of her Minou, Minimouche, or le Petit Prince.

Julia never lost her yen for travel, and wherever she went, cats were bound to turn up—sometimes in unexpected places. For several years she was invited to teach a cooking class at the luxe Hotel Cipriani in Venice, a dazzling resort across from the Piazza San Marco, where water taxis plied the canals, ferrying guests from museums to restaurants to shops and back again. The French Chef could still attract a fervent following of well-heeled Americans just by doing what she loved the most—cooking good food and making it fun. Without Paul, her lifelong helpmate, she asked two dear

friends from Cambridge, Pat and Herb Pratt, to go along and assist with the demonstrations.

One night, strolling home across the bridge after a glorious dinner, Julia tripped and fell, but picked herself up and insisted on enjoying the rest of the evening. It soon became clear that her injuries, including a badly cut lip, needed medical attention, so the hotel staff helped Julia and her friends into a water taxi headed for the nearest *pronto soccorso*. By the time they arrived it was pitch dark and the fifteenth-century *castello*'s colonnades were dimly lit, but Julia was wide awake and typically curious.

She settled into a wheelchair for the ride through the silent courtyard to the far side of the hospital for X-rays. From the murky shadows, one, then two, then six cats peeped out from behind mossy columns and formed a disorganized but attentive escort. White-coated attendants seemed unfazed by cats wandering around a hospital, and though most Americans would be taken aback, Julia thought feline candy stripers were the perfect cheerer-uppers. The *dottore* offered no anesthesia before stitching her lip, but Julia didn't mind. She stoically endured the procedure, entertained by the serenade of six *gatto* tenors pacing outside the treatment room.

On a visit to Paris, Julia and the Pratts attended an elegant dinner party in the Palais Bourbon, a fashionable neighborhood not far from the old Roo de Loo apartment. Ten guests were seated around a large round table, and when the hostess went to the kitchen to check on dessert, the family cat ambled into the room and leaped onto her chair. Looking around smartly and brightly, the pussycat seemed to follow the witty comments of the guests, as if about to contribute a bon meow or two to the conversation.

No one paid much attention to the cat ensconced at the head of the table, but Julia was elated by her new dining companion. When the hostess returned to reclaim her seat, the puss with savoir faire to spare relinquished his place and, with what appeared to be a feline Gallic shrug, settled on his corner ottoman.

For Julia the recipe for a perfect dinner party had just been greatly enhanced: fine food, plentiful wine, sparkling conversation, and a cat who came to dinner.

Julia meets a Venetian friend

"DO I LOOK retiring?" Julia bristled when reporters called her Montecito home a retirement community. Slowed by three back operations for a pinched nerve but still high-spirited, she learned to manipulate a walker and cane, and waited impatiently for visitors to whisk her away to wherever there were interesting people and something good to eat.

Heads turned when she cruised grocery aisles, squeezing, sniffing, and marveling over a new variety of lettuce or a perfect Comice pear she just had to bite into on the spot. Once word got out that *Julia* was in the house, a horde of shoppers would queue up at a respectful distance, robotically filling their carts with whatever she was buying.

She was a Saturday morning regular at the bustling farmers' market in downtown Santa Barbara that reminded her of the cacophonous open-air stalls in Cannes. She beamed at the sight of so many zealous converts to the gospel of good eating, who hunted for the perfect artichoke and toe-*mah*-toes picked just hours ago. She stopped to chat with the orange man and the cucumber woman and nibbled nonstop. When she tasted a perfectly ripe strawberry, the surge of pleasure registered on her face as vividly as it did fifty years before when she trolled the markets of Paris.

Julia slung her bags of goodies over the handlebars of her walker and, when she tired, turned it around and plopped onto the makeshift stool to catch her breath. A few supplicants would approach and ask her to sign something. "How wonderful to see you!" "My kids eat green beans because you showed me how to cook them." She basked in the attention.

On one trip her shopping companion bought a plastic pot of bright green shoots that Julia didn't recognize. It turned out to be "kitty grass," a digestive aid for her cat. Julia immediately wanted to know everything about this cat: How old, how big, how fluffy, how playful? Any pictures? She confided that she loved poussiequettes so much, she would have become a feline vet, if she hadn't discovered French food first.

Julia's ninetieth birthday prompted a string of glamorous galas, most of them fund-raisers for her favorite causes—anything to advance culinary education. Lavish dinners honoring the "Queen of Cuisine" were prepared by some of the country's premier chefs, and included a $500-a-plate supper in the Napa Valley, an elegant French buffet at the Smithsonian, and a five-course, all-lobster dinner (except for dessert) in Boston. She relished them all, but her tastes now ran to less fancy fare. She still looked forward to lunching at fine restaurants, especially when the chef cooked up something she had a taste for, like a bowl of New England clam chowder. She was grateful when her chef friend Jim Dodge periodically filled the freezer with mini gourmet dinners she could defrost for guests. Friends were always happy to hear Julia's voice on their answering machines with a cheery invitation to dinner and her signature sign-off, "Meow!"

Julia always saw herself as a serious home cook rather than a chef. When food talk got too precious, she mischievously called it "kweezeen." She dismissed fad diets and the "food police" who would ban butter, cream, and red meat, spreading fear of food throughout the land. She adored Chinese food because it reminded her of those dinners in Kunming when she and Paul were falling in love, and she often had a hankering for braised ribs, peanut butter, and her "reverse martinis"—one

Extra brut, with just a whisker of catnip

part gin to seven parts vermouth. She raved about the hot dogs at Costco.

Julia treated special out-of-towners to her personal tour of Santa Barbara. First stop, the In-N-Out Burger. One friend swore Julia knew every one between Santa Barbara and San Francisco, though she preferred the *pommes frites* at the Golden Arches. Julia and company got their burgers and fries to go and picnicked on the beach with a breathtaking view of the Pacific. After lunch the tour wound through the center of town, past the landmark hundred-year-old fig tree, and sometimes took a side trip to the zoo, to visit the Really Big Cats, of course.

Finally, the car stopped in front of the star attraction as Julia trilled brightly, "Now we're all going to visit the Cat House," an announcement that never failed to raise eyebrows. She led them toward a rambling old Victorian with an odd structure in the yard that housed a forest of cat trees, carpeted kitty condos, meandering catwalks, and a kitty infirmary. The whole place undulated with pussycats— prowling, tumbling, napping, stretching, and purring for attention. A haven for three hundred homeless cats, and heaven for Julia.

Julia merrily greeted the shelter's owner and pushed her walker through the meowing maze as cats crowded around, rubbing at her ankles. She stooped to pet her favorites, cuddled a few lucky ones, and asked to meet the latest arrivals. Her tour guests usually headed for the car long before Julia was ready to bid the poussiequettes *"Au revoir. À bientôt!"* Even non-cat people had to admit that the scene was delightfully wacky, but so utterly Julia.

HER *ESPRIT* WAS willing, but at ninety-one the bum knees Julia blamed on her basketball days at Smith finally gave out. She struggled to get around in her small townhouse even with a cane and walker, so she determined to have knee replacement surgery. Soon after the painful operation, one of her favorite lunch companions asked what they put in there when they removed her kneecap. Eyes twinkling, she whispered, "Oh, Jim, just a little bouquet garni."

Sometimes it was difficult to summon that twinkle. When her days lacked zest she'd ask to go for long drives along the hilly roads dotted with avocado farms and lemon groves. Ocean breezes carried the scent of lilies and lavender. Roses too—she favored butter-yellow ones, like the bushes she and Paul had nurtured in Provence and Cambridge. The waves of rainbow-hued fields and distant mountains stirred memories of la Peetch and the surrounding countryside that produced blossoms by the ton for French perfumeries. The twisted trunks of olive trees reminded her of the one that grew near their stone patio, a bower for sleepy poussiequettes. Swaying palms, cypress, and hot-pink bougainvillea made her ask, "Are you *sure* we're not in France?"

Something else released a flood of memories. If you looked—and she always did—there were country cats chasing mice from the winery floor, threading rows of citrus trees, or rolling in tall grass. She recalled the parade of kitties who wore a path between her kitchen and Simca's. And her cherished poussiequettes: Minimouche, Minouche, le Petit Prince, Whiskey-Minoir, even the naughty Minimere. She missed them all.

Her *maison* was still *sans chat*, and she wasn't happy about
it. Then, voilà! A friend showed up one day with a special
delivery: a tiny black-and-white kitten with a wild look in its
eye. Something about this little imp beguiled Julia. It nipped
at her heels, crashed into her walker, snagged her sweaters,
and gave too many little love bites. Julia called him—what
else?—Minou. Whether he would answer to that, or at all, was
another story.

A teensy thing with supersized curiosity, Minou soon
wiggled his way into every cupboard, closet, and corner. Often,

after searching under bedcovers and piles of papers, she might find him curled in a coffee cup or soup bowl. Minou chased butterflies, and his tail, in the small enclosed patio, but was soon scaling the wall to see what lay beyond, though he always came home when dinner was served.

For the mischief-loving Julia, it added to the fun that the kitten was a forbidden pleasure. Pets were banished from the upscale Montecito complex, but Julia blithely dismissed the rules and insisted, "My cat's not going to bother anybody." Even in so-called retirement she was the most interesting thing to happen around there in years, with or without her little outlaw.

Julia had underestimated her kitten's spunk. He specialized in surprise attacks, waiting in the bushes for Julia's neighbors to wheel their walkers deliberately past the house, in hopes of spotting the famous resident. Mighty Minou would stalk, crouch, and launch like a heat-seeking missile toward his hapless victim. Startled cries and meows brought the housekeeper rushing to the rescue, with Julia trailing behind. Captivated by the familiar fluty voice, the neighbor happily accepted an apology—"So sorry, dearie!"—and an invitation to meet in the dining room for breakfast with Julia, *sans* pussycat.

When Minou tired of his game of "gotcha" with the slow-moving prey, he'd come inside and nestle against Julia's chest while she read the local paper. Occasionally he'd halfheartedly reach up to scratch the page or paw at her bifocals, but usually settled into a sleepy purring ball. He soon timed his naps to coincide with hers and claimed a spot on the pillow beside her head. Day and night, Julia and her poussiequette were inseparable.

THE PARTY IN THE KITCHEN

ON A SUNNY August day a week before she died, Julia posed for a snapshot near the door to her flower-filled patio. She is impeccably dressed as always, her bright eyes gaze into the lens. In her lap she holds her frisky black kitten, white paws momentarily at rest.

The image echoes one Paul took of Julia and Minette in their Roo de Loo apartment a half century earlier. The same smartly dressed figure, forthright look, and hands fondly wrapped around her first feline love.

Paul's Paris photo captured the fresh-faced California bride who had just discovered France and food and poussiequettes, poised at the threshold of a whole new life. The last one revealed an unlikely revolutionary, a woman who had lived long enough to see the transformative effect of her passion and perseverance. Her secret was a gift for connecting, inviting everyone to the party in the kitchen and making it the liveliest, coolest place in the house. Up to her elbows in cake flour or waving a slippery chicken at the camera, she reminded everyone of the goal, singing, "Above all, have a good time. *Bon appétit!*" Americans wholeheartedly embraced her message that the party is life itself, that cooking and eating well are essential to happiness.

Festive plans were well under way when Julia died peacefully in her sleep, two days shy of her ninety-second

Julia with Minou, August 2004

Julia and Minette in Paris

birthday. Friends and family gathered anyway, knowing that Julia would never let anything get in the way of a celebration. So they poured vintage wine and clinked glasses, sounding the "bells of friendship" as they repeated Paul and Julia's favorite toast, "*le carillon de l'amitie*." The highlight of their feast was a white chocolate and Italian buttercream cake, topped with peaches and sweet reminiscences. Favorite Julia stories flowed through the laughter and tears.

Julia's niece, Dorothy's daughter, thought the McWilliams sisters of Pasadena—two tall, smart, funny, strong-willed, merrymaking, and pussycat-loving women—should rest together, so she mingled their ashes and returned to Paris and the old *hôtel particulier* at 81 rue de l'Université.

There was the balcony where Julia, often with Minette in her arms, had looked out over the rooftops of Paris and felt a surge of excitement and love for the city and people who opened their hearts to her. Julia once said, "I just get a lift of sheer happiness every time I look out of the window."

She sprinkled the ashes under a tree, returning Julia to her true home—*la belle France*—as central to her idea of heaven on earth as Paul, food, and the company of cats.

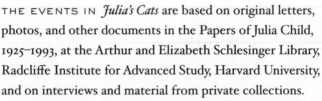

THE EVENTS IN *Julia's Cats* are based on original letters, photos, and other documents in the Papers of Julia Child, 1925–1993, at the Arthur and Elizabeth Schlesinger Library, Radcliffe Institute for Advanced Study, Harvard University, and on interviews and material from private collections.

All quotations in the text are from Julia's letters, Paul Child's letter-diary to his twin brother, Charles Child, from 1948 to 1977, and the personal correspondence of Julia Child with Simone (Simca) Beck et al. from 1965 to 1982. Simca's letters to Julia have been translated from the French by the authors. We are grateful to the Julia Child Foundation for Gastronomy and the Culinary Arts and to the Schlesinger Library for permission to publish these excerpts from the collection.

ADDITIONAL SOURCE NOTES

p. 6   Julia responded to many requests for "a last meal"; this description is based on a column by restaurateur George Lang and quoted in Laura Shapiro, *Julia Child: A Life* (New York: Viking Penguin, 2007), 175. Julia's actual last meal: interview, Stephanie Hersh.

p. 22   Colette at the Palais Royal: Julia Child with Alex Prud'homme, *My Life in France* (New York: Knopf, 2006), 52–53.

p. 58   Presents first Cordon Bleu dinner with cat on her shoulder: Noël Riley Fitch, *Appetite for Life: The Biography of Julia Child* (New York: Anchor Books, 1999), 175.

p. 61   Mrs. Child did "not have any great natural talent for cooking.": Fitch, 180.

p. 66   "Maybe the cat has fallen into the stew . . .": Child and Prud'homme, 71.

p. 81   Julia and Simca's shared cat: Simone Beck with Suzanne Patterson, *Food and Friends: Recipes and Memories from Simca's Cuisine* (New York: Penguin, 1991), 300.

p. 114   "Paul Child, the man who is always there . . .": Julia Child, *The French Chef Cookbook* (New York: Knopf, 1968), xvi.

p. 128   Julia might have become a feline vet: Lisa McKinnon, "To Market with Julia," *Ventura County Star*, March 3, 2003, http://www.vcstar.com/news/2002/Mar/03/to-market-with-julia, accessed March 12, 2012, quoted with author's permission.

ACKNOWLEDGMENTS

EVENTS IN JULIA'S later years in Cambridge and California are based on interviews with family, friends, and colleagues. Cat people or not, they agreed that telling Julia's life's story in the company of cats would be "jolly good fun." It has been that, and so much more. We count ourselves lucky to have spent time with those who knew her so well and would like to thank them all for enriching our understanding of this extraordinary woman.

SPECIAL THANKS TO:

Philadelphia Cousins, Julia's devoted niece and trustee of the Julia Child Foundation, offered guidance throughout our research and encouraged others to share their stories. David McWilliams told us what it was like to live in Aunt Julia's Cambridge house during graduate school and, later, to take the "Julia tour" of Santa Barbara that began with burgers on the beach and ended with visits to a quirky Cat House.

Stephanie Hersh, Julia's personal assistant and companion of sixteen years, whose stories revealed the texture of Julia's daily life and the laughter they shared. Pat Pratt and husband Herb traveled with the Childs and belonged to their Cambridge circle. Spending time with Pat, it's easy to see why these two vibrant and witty Smith College alums would be lifelong best friends.

Jim Dodge, master chef and "chauffeur," who outfitted his red pickup with special running boards to accommodate Julia. He brightened many of her California days, and ours as well with his insights and encouragement, and asserted, "If you don't know how much Julia loved cats, you didn't know Julia." Maggie Mah Johnson, Julia's multitalented culinary assistant, graciously shared her collection of photos and memorabilia and her fond recollections. She and Sandy Shepard illuminated Julia's friendship with Rosemary Manell, a fascinating woman in her own right who deserves more space than we were able to give. Sandy trusted us with boxes containing a lifetime of Rosemary's mementos and letters between the Manells and Childs, and sent us on our way with a vintage bottle from Rosie's wine cellar.

Rebecca Alssid, cofounder with Julia and Jacques Pépin of a unique master's program in gastronomy at Boston University, reminisced about Santa Barbara visits with her still-exuberant friend. David Nussbaum, Julia's cookbook collaborator and cat-loving friend, offered glimpses of Julia in action before the cameras, and the precious photo of Julia with her last kitten, Minou. Linda Carucci, Patty McWilliams, Marian Morash, Kim Schwartz, and others who shared their memories. *Grosses bises à tous!*

Many people helped us navigate the archives: Very special praise to Diana Carey, reference librarian for visual resources at the Schlesinger Library, who tirelessly tracked down photos and documents while ongoing cataloging made the collection a moving target. She, Lynda Leahy, and the Reading Room staff, who are as gracious as they are efficient, made hunting through boxes of manuscripts a pleasure. Thanks to Ellen M. Shea, head of research services at the Schlesinger, and Susy Davidson, executive director of the Julia Child Foundation, for facilitating the permissions process.

Merci beaucoup! David Cashion, our editor at Abrams, who instantly got the spirit of this book, helped give it form, and nurtured it with care, and to Darilyn Carnes for her stylish and elegant design. To our agent, Claire Gerus, whose support and sage advice put us on track for what has been a fascinating ride. To our faithful friends, especially Peggy Hughes, Susan Prince, and Jo Bolger, who came running when we were stumped by the vagaries of Microsoft or just needed encouragement over a glass of whine. And to the memory of Margie and her Minou.

Finally, to Julia and all the poussiequettes who put the *joie* in her joie de vivre. Her secret to the good life was simple: Find something you love and do it every day. For us that something was writing *Julia's Cats*.

PATRICIA BAREY AND THERESE BURSON own a media production company whose programs have won top honors at major international competitions.

Ms. Barey received Emmys for public television profiles of Chicago's food and restaurant scene and the pioneering work of Dr. Elisabeth Kübler-Ross. She lives in Tucson, Arizona, with two *chats lunatiques*, Ella and Rosie.

Ms. Burson, who holds a PhD in English, taught college literature, wrote scripts for national PBS series on the environment and school desegregation, and produced an award-winning documentary about the Art Institute of Chicago. She lives in Evanston, Illinois, in a *maison* currently *sans chat*.

Throughout the writing of this book, they found sustenance and inspiration in their butter-stained copies of Julia's masterful cookbooks.

For more information about *Julia's Cats*, visit juliascats.com.

JULIA CHILD'S RECIPE FOR *LANGUES-DE-CHAT* (CAT'S TONGUE COOKIES)

These crisp little wafers go with ice creams and fruit desserts, and are wonderful to have on hand when you want a molded magnificence, since you can use them rather than ladyfingers. They freeze perfectly, too, so you might make a lot while you're at it.

For about 30 cookies, 4 inches long and 1¼ to 1½ inches wide

½ stick (2 ounces) soft unsalted butter
⅓ cup sugar
The grated rind of 1 lemon
¼ cup egg whites (about 2 "large" egg whites)
⅓ cup all-purpose flour (measure by scooping dry-measure cup into flour
    and sweeping off excess)

Equipment. 2 or more buttered and floured cookie sheets, the largest you have, and no-stick recommended; a 12- to 14-inch pastry bag with ⅜-inch round tube opening; a flour sifter set over wax paper; an electric beater or wooden spoon; a rubber spatula and a flexible-blade spatula; a cake rack.

Preliminaries. Preheat oven to 425 degrees and set racks in upper- and lower-middle levels. Prepare pastry sheets, assemble pastry bag, and set out all your ingredients and equipment.

The batter. The mixture here is only butter and sugar beaten to a pommade (a light and fluffy consistency), then mixed with plain egg white, and finally with flour; the trick is to keep it light and fluffy so it has enough body to hold in a pastry bag and be squeezed out. Proceed as follows: Using an electric beater or a wooden spoon, whip the butter, sugar, and grated lemon rind in a small bowl until they form a fluffy pommade—if you have softened it too much and it has turned limp and almost liquid, beat over ice water to bring it back to a fluffy, almost foamy, state. Beat the egg whites briefly with a fork, just to break them up. Pour ½ tablespoon of them into the butter-sugar mixture and rapidly cut it in with a rubber spatula, giving 3 or 4 brief scoops. Do not try to mix thoroughly because you do not want to soften the batter; rapidly cut in the rest of the egg whites by ½ tablespoons. Then sift on one quarter of the flour, rapidly cut it into the mixture, and continue with the rest in small portions. Stand the pastry bag in a cup, spread the top open, and scoop in the batter.

Forming the cookies. Using quick straight strokes, form lines of the batter on the prepared cookie sheets, making lines 3 to 4 inches long and the width of your finger, spaced 3 inches apart—they will spread in the oven.

Baking. Bake 2 sheets at a time in upper- and lower-middle levels of pre-heated 425-degree oven. In 6 to 8 minutes, when ⅛ inch around their circumference has browned, the cookies are done. Remove from oven and immediately, with a flexible-blade spatula, dislodge cookies onto a rack. They will crisp as they cool.

*Store in a warming oven, or wrap airtight and freeze.